AM

F

FLAME OF LOVE

D1002995

Visit our web site at
www.albahouse.org
(for orders www.alba-house.com)

or call 1-800-343-2522 (ALBA)
and request current catalog

Flame *of* *Love*

POEMS OF THE SPANISH MYSTICS

San Juan de la Cruz (St. John of the Cross)

Santa Teresa de Jesús (St. Teresa of Avila)

English Translation by Loren G. Smith

ST PAULS

Alba
House

Library of Congress Cataloging-in-Publication Data

Flame of love : poems of the Spanish mystics / San Juan de la Cruz (St. John of the Cross), Santa Teresa de Jesús (St. Teresa of Avila) ; English translation by Elegies.
    p. cm.
    ISBN 0-8189-0977-3
1. John of the Cross, Saint, 1542-1591—Translations into English. 2. Teresa, of Avila, Saint, 1515-1582—Translations into English. 3. Spanish poetry—Classical period, 1500-1700—Translations into English. 4. Religious poetry, Spanish—Translations into English. 5. Mysticism—Poetry. I. Smith, Loren G. (Loren Glenn) II. John of the Cross, Saint, 1542-1591. Poems. English & Spanish. Selections. III. Teresa, of Avila, Saint, 1515-1582. Poems. English & Spanish. Selections.
    PQ6400.J8A235 2005
    861'.30803824822—dc22
                        2005010978

ELEGIES is the pseudonym of Loren G. Smith

Produced and designed in the United States of America by the
Fathers and Brothers of the Society of St. Paul,
2187 Victory Boulevard, Staten Island, New York 10314-6603,
as part of their communications apostolate.

ISBN: 0-8189-0977-3

Printing Information:

Current Printing - first digit	1	2	3	4	5	6	7	8	9	10

Year of Current Printing - first year shown

2005	2006	2007	2008	2009	2010	2011	2012	2013

To Joan,
Chris, Polly,
and their families
for whom the Flame of Love
will burn within my heart forever;

and special thanks to Norm Shapiro for his
encouragement, instructions and improvements;

and to Susan Muto for the wisdom of her writings
and her support of this project from its early stages.

Table of Contents

SAINT TERESA OF AVILA

Foreword

by Susan Muto, Ph.D.

Dean, Epiphany Academy of Formative Spirituality
Pittsburgh, Pennsylvania

Over the years I have been privileged to read several drafts of the poetic translations that comprise this elegant work of love, now in a book of its own. The author has poured into each line of poetry the affection he feels for these two great Spanish mystics, John of the Cross and Teresa of Avila.

Trying to capture the exquisite rhythm and music of their original poetic meditations in the English language was a daunting task, guided every step of the way by divine grace. One can imagine the author ruminating upon each word, each line, image, symbol, phrase and metaphor, to capture their meaning and their mystery.

This is the kind of poetry one reads not once but many times over. Certain lines will never be forgotten. As we know, long before a commentary on his poetry was written, Saint John of the Cross heard the music of eternity in his heart and wrote it down for future generations to share. As we read in a poem like "Entering a Place Unknown," it is impossible to capture adequately what it means to be lifted up by the mystery to the highest reaches of transcendent luminosity.

As Saint John writes in this new translation, "I now knew the narrow way; / such a secret way to pray / left me stammering at the ending,/ *all my knowledge far transcending.*"

Less known both in Spanish and English is the poetry of Saint Teresa of Avila. The author has done us a great service by bringing her work as a poet to the attention of readers who have already been inspired by the story of her life and works of genius like *The Interior Castle*. We rejoice in reading such convictions as "How happy the heart that by love is elated, / in which only God all its thought has embraced, / renouncing for him every thing that's created, / and finding its glory and joy by him graced."

I would urge discriminating readers of this exquisite work to go slowly, to dwell upon and savor each work, to let the music carry them from their lips into their mind and down deep into their heart. This is a poetry that forms and transforms our lives. It is not to be read once but many times over until it becomes as much a part of our life of intimacy with God a it was for John and Teresa. With these masters by our side we all wish for the grace to pray:

> Let nothing disturb you,
> let nothing affright you,
> for everything passes,
> and God is unchanging,
> through Patience
> all things are obtained;
> who holds fast to God
> finds nothing is lacking.
> God solely suffices.

Introduction

San Juan de la Cruz (Saint John of the Cross) is regarded as one of the greatest poets of the Spanish language and among the greatest mystical poets of any language. Born Juan de Yepes in Castile, Spain in 1542, he was raised in poverty, but received a good education in the classics from the Jesuits. John entered the Carmelite order at the age of 21, continuing his studies in theology and scholastic philosophy at Salamanca, one of Europe's leading universities, where he was regarded as an outstanding student.

Drawn to the contemplative life, he was recruited in 1567 by Teresa de Jesús (St. Teresa of Avila) to participate in her reform of the discalced Carmelites. Teresa became John's teacher, mentor and protector. In 1577, these reform activities resulted in John's imprisonment for nine months by adversaries within the order. While suffering from terrible conditions and treatment, he began to compose some of his most beautiful, passionate poetry including the *Spiritual Canticle*. Following his escape from prison, he completed this poem and went on to write the two others for which he is most famous, *Dark Night* and *Living Flame of Love*, along with their companion prose texts which are still considered among the most profound guides to the spiritual life ever written.

John died of illness in 1591, at the age of 49. He was canonized in 1726, and declared a Doctor of the Church in 1926. In 1952, the Spanish Ministry of National Education named John of the Cross the patron of Spanish poets.

Santa Teresa de Jesús (Saint Teresa of Avila) was born Teresa Sánchez de Cepeda y Ahumada in 1515, in Avila, Spain of the aristocratic class. In 1535, she entered the Carmelite monastery in Avila.

Teresa's fame rests on her extraordinary accomplishments in the reform of the Carmelite order and the founding and administration of new monasteries (overcoming intense opposition and chronic health problems); on her prose writings which have remained among the most popular and valuable guides to the spiritual life; and on the sanctity of her life, attaining the highest degrees of prayer and contemplation with John of the Cross as her spiritual director.

She died in 1582, at the age of 67, and was canonized in 1622. In 1970, Teresa became the first woman to be declared a Doctor of the Church.

About the Poetry

John considered his poetry to be the most authentic expression of his theology and his ineffable mystical experience. Poetry is the language of the heart and soul. Prose, the language of the mind, best conveys the linear, rational, factual expression of the things we have mastered — the truth we can define. Poetry better communicates the deep emotions — love, loss, suffering and joy — the things that have mastered us — the Truth we know but can't describe — the eternal paradox that encompasses the "reality" of our lives. Common themes in John's poetry include comprehending through unknowing, illumination through obscureness of the dark night, and the delightful healing wounds from the Holy Spirit's living flame of love within him.

Above all, John's poetry speaks of love — the infinite and unconditional love that his Beloved first gave to attract its loved one; then nourished within his heart to achieve a perfect union between the lovers. Interestingly, the first three poems in this text, which have won universal recognition as being among the greatest love poems ever written, make no use of traditional religious language beyond the rich imagery borrowed from the Song of Songs.

John's poems were written years before his prose commentaries, which are based on three of those poems, providing an explanation of their meaning and their implications for spiritual growth and understanding of mystical theology. The poems can be enjoyed without reference to the commentaries and it is generally recommended that readers start with the poems and let them speak for themselves. For those wishing to learn more about the author and his writings, ICS Publications' *The Collected Works of St. John of the Cross* provides all of the text, well annotated, along with excellent introductory materials (available online at: www.icspublications.org). Readers unfamiliar with this form of religious writing should consider starting with John's commentaries on *The Living Flame of Love* and *The Spiritual Canticle* prior to tackling *The Ascent of Mt. Carmel* and *The Dark Night*. While the latter two can be invaluable guides to spiritual growth, especially for those who find themselves becoming disillusioned with the materialistic life, their emphasis on the ascetical can be difficult for today's readers to appreciate. It is important to understand that the mystic is drawn by the experience of God's love to desire holiness, and that ascetical practices (which have varied in different ages and cultures) are an expression of this. It is love that creates the mystic, not hair shirts and fasting. This message is most clearly communicated by *Flame* and *Canticle*. Contemporary commentaries on these texts can be very helpful, phrasing his concepts in more familiar language and demonstrating their relevance to modern life. Susan Muto has written an excellent set of companion texts for each of John's prose works (available at: www.epiphanyassociation.org).

Teresa's poetry, unlike John's, is not integrally tied to her prose writings or the exposition of her mystical theology. Nor has it received the same acclaim and attention. But, similar to John, she used poetry as a way of expressing the ineffable — an outpouring of the intense feelings and desires inspired by that divine flame of love which consumed her. Teresa speaks of this in *The Book of Her Life* (chap. 14,4): "Oh, help me God! What is the soul like when it is in this state! It would want to be all tongues so as to praise the Lord. It speaks folly in a thousand holy ways, ever trying to find means of pleasing the one who thus possesses it. I know a person who though not a poet suddenly composed some deeply-felt verses well expressing her pain. They were not composed by the use of her intellect; rather, in order that she enjoy the glory so delightful a distress gave to her, she complained of it in this way to God. She desired all her body and soul to break in pieces to demonstrate the joy she felt in this pain." Her poetry expresses the emotions that all lovers feel: adoration, joy, desire, pain over the beloved's absence, impatience to remove all obstacles that separate the lovers — and in the special case of the mystic a longing for death to attain perfect union with the Beloved. This should not be confused with a desire to take one's own life, since above all the love of a true mystic inspires the desire to serve and obey God's will. See Philippians 1:19-26 for St. Paul's discussion of this. Toward the end of her life Teresa, discussing the final stage of spiritual growth in *The Interior Castle* (7th dwelling place, chap. 3), makes it clear that she now no longer desired to die, but would rather live many years with much suffering if that would serve God better.

Teresa also composed poetry to instruct the sisters of her monasteries with her profound insights about spiritual and religious life. But we also know from the writings of Teresa and others that she enjoyed writing verses spontaneously and sharing them with her companions. She took particular delight when her sisters would set them to music. The poems of both Teresa and John were frequently sung by nuns and monks to celebrate liturgical feasts, or simply for their own enjoyment. Teresa's approach to reforming the Carmelite order sought to balance an increased focus on contemplation, solitude and detachment from material concerns with moderation in austerities and emphasis on Christian joy, encouraging recreation and the sharing of song and poetry. Unfortunately much, if not most, of the poetry of Teresa and John has not been preserved; but what we have can be a source of wisdom, comfort and joy to us as well.

The objective in preparing these English versions has been to provide the most accurate possible translation while retaining the original rhyming schemes and utilizing meters as close to the original as possible. Preserving the meaning of the original poems has been given priority over aesthetic considerations.

Spanish versions of these poems are from *The Collected Works of St. John of the Cross* and *The Collected Works of St. Teresa of Avila*, ICS Publications, Institute of Carmelite Studies, Washington, D.C.

San Juan de la Cruz

(Saint John of the Cross)

Llama de Amor Viva

¡Oh llama de amor viva,
que tiernamente hieres
de mi alma en el más profundo centro!
Pues ya no eres esquiva,
acaba ya, si quieres;
¡rompe la tela de este dulce encuentro!

¡Oh cauterio suave!
¡Oh regalada llaga!
¡Oh mano blanda! ¡Oh toque delicado,
que a vida eterna sabe,
y toda deuda paga!
Matando, muerte en vida la has trocado.

¡Oh lamparas de fuego,
en cuyos resplandores
las profundas cavernas del sentido,
que estaba oscuro y ciego,
con extraños primores
calor y luz dan junto a su Querido!

¡Cuán manso y amoroso
recuerdas en mi seno,
donde secretamente solo moras,
y en tu aspirar sabroso,
de bien y gloria lleno,
cuán delicadamente me enamoras!

Living Flame of Love

O living flame of love
whose tender burning fire
wounds sore my soul within its deepest center!
No more depriving of
completing your desire,
now burst the veil, perfect this sweet encounter!

O cautery's mellow glow!
O healing wound's delight!
O gentle hand! Oh delicate touch, you taste
of heavenly life, and lo!
each debt is set aright!
You killed, yet with new life my death you graced.

O lamps of fiery light,
within whose radiant splendor
the very deepest caverns of my sense,
once dark, bereft of sight,
now with rare beauty render
to Lover light and ardor full intense!

How soft your love's sensations,
that waken in my heart,
where only you alone in secret live;
and your sweet inspirations
all good and glory impart,
as tenderly the grace of love you give!

Noche Oscura

En una noche oscura
con ansias, en amores inflamada,
¡oh dichosa ventura!
salí sin ser notada
estando ya mi casa sosegada.

A oscura y segura,
por la secreta escala disfrazada,
¡oh dichosa ventura!
a oscuras y en celada,
estando ya mi casa sosegada.

En la noche dichosa,
en secreto, que nadie me veía,
ni yo miraba cosa,
sin otra luz y guía
sino la que en el corazón ardía.

Aquésta me guiaba
más cierto que la luz del mediodía,
adónde me esperaba
quien yo bien me sabía,
en parte donde nadie parecía.

Dark Night

Deep in the dark of night
with yearning, set aflame by love's own fire,
— oh, happy grace-full flight! —
I left with no descrier,
as all my household, peaceful, would retire.

Secure, out of the light,
disguised, up secret ladder ever higher,
— oh, happy grace-full flight! —
the dark hid my desire,
as all my household, peaceful, would retire.

Within that happy night,
in secret, without anyone's discerning,
nor aught that caught my sight,
nor guide nor light returning
save for the one that in my heart was burning.

It served me as my guide,
more certain than the brilliant midday sun,
to where for me would bide —
how well I knew! — the One,
where we might not be found by anyone.

¡Oh noche que guiaste!
¡Oh noche amable más que el alborada!
¡Oh noche que juntaste
Amado con amada,
amada en el Amado transformada!

En mi pecho florido,
que entero para él solo se guardaba,
allí quedó dormido,
y yo le regalaba,
y el ventalle de cedros aire daba.

El aire de la almena,
cuando yo sus cabellos esparcía,
con su mano serena
en mi cuello hería
y todos mis sentidos suspendía.

Quedéme y olvidéme,
el rostro recliné sobre el Amado,
cesó todo y dejéme,
dejando me cuidado
entre las azucenas olvidado.

O night that guides my flight!
O night that was more loving than the sun!
O night that would unite
the Lover and loved one,
beloved changed to Lover — unison!

Upon my blossoming breast —
I guarded it for only him, no less —
there he remained at rest,
I gave him my caress,
our love the fanning cedars' breeze would bless.

The breeze blew from the tower,
my fingers now began to part his hair,
with his hand's gentle power
he wounded my neck where
my senses, stricken, faded unaware.

I lost, forgot my being,
my face reclined upon my Lover there;
all ceased, my spirit freeing,
and leaving all my care
behind, forgotten, midst the lilies fair.

Cantico Espiritual

(*Esposa*)
¿Adonde te escondiste,
Amado, y me dejaste con gemido?
Como el ciervo huiste,
habiéndome herido;
salí tras ti clamando, y eras ido.

Pastores, los que fuerdes
allá, por las majadas al otero,
si por ventura vierdes
aquel que yo más quiero,
decilde que adolezco, peno y muero.

Buscando mis amores,
iré por esos montes y riberas;
ni cogeré las flores,
ni temeré las fieras,
y pasaré los fuertes y fronteras.

¡Oh bosques y espesuras,
plantadas por la mano del Amado!
¡Oh prado de verduras,
de flores esmaltado,
decid si por vosotros ha pasado!

Spiritual Canticle (second redaction)

(Bride)
Where have you hid from sight,
Beloved, leaving me behind to groan?
Gone like the stag in flight,
you gored me to the bone;
I chased you, calling, and was left alone.

You shepherds on the height,
there, through the sheep-folds climbing to the hill,
by chance if you should sight
the one I yearn for, will
you say I'm sick, in pain, enough to kill.

To find my love I'll scour
through every river bank and mountain tier,
and stop to pick no flower,
let wild beasts cause no fear,
and pass beyond each strong man and frontier.

O thickets, groves of trees,
by my Beloved's hand you all were born!
O peaceful verdant leas,
his flowers now adorn,
pray tell me if he passed you by this morn!

Mil gracias derramando,
pasó por estos sotos con presura,
e, yéndolos mirando,
con sola su figura,
vestidos los dejó de hermosura.

¡Ay, quién podrá sanarme!
¡Acaba de entregarte ya de vero;
no quieras enviarme
de hoy más ya mensajero
que no saben decirme lo que quiero!

Y todos cuantos vagan
de ti me van mil gracias refiriendo,
y todos más me llagan,
y déjeme muriendo
un no sé qué quedan balbuciendo.

Mas, ¿como perseveras,
¡oh vida!, no viviendo donde vives,
y haciendo porque mueras
las flechas que recibes
de lo que del Amado en ti concibes?

¿Por qué, pues has llagado
aqueste corazón, no le sanaste?
Y, pues me le has robado,
¿por qué así le dejaste,
y no tomas el robo que robaste?

He spread a thousand graces,
while traveling through these wooded groves with speed,
and, looking on these places,
his image filled the need
to leave them clothed in beauty fair indeed.

Ah, who can serve to mend me!
Surrender now yourself to me I pray;
do not attempt to send me
a messenger from this day
who cannot tell what I want him to say.

From all who wander past,
reminders come of all your thousand graces,
each wounds more than the last,
puts me in death's embraces,
that know-not-what beyond their babbling faces.

How do you persevere,
O life!, not living where you live, I grieve,
the closer death comes near
from arrows you receive
from what of your Beloved you conceive?

Why cause this injury
to my heart, then refuse to make it heal?
You stole that heart from me,
why scorn the pain I feel,
and not retain the thing that you did steal?

¡Apaga mis enojos,
pues que ninguno basta a deshacellos,
y véante mis ojos,
pues eres lumbre de ellos,
y sólo para ti quiero tenellos!

Descubre tu presencia,
y máteme tu vista y hermosura.
Mira que la dolencia
de amor, que no se cura
sino con la presencia y la figura.

¡Oh cristalina fuente,
si en esos tus semblantes plateados
formases de repente
los ojos deseados
que tengo en mis entrañas dibujados!

¡Apártalos, Amado,
que voy de vuelo!
  (*Esposo*)
— Vuélvate, paloma,
que el ciervo vulnerado
por el otero asoma
al aire de tu vuelo, y fresco toma!
  (*Esposa*)
Mi Amado, las montañas,
los valles solitarios nemorosos,
las ínsulas extrañas,
los ríos sonorosos,
el silbo de los aires amorosos,

Relieve my passionate sighs,
there is no other who can ease my plight,
show yourself to my eyes,
you are their only light,
for you alone I wish to have their sight!

Reveal your presence to me,
your vision and beauty now my death procure.
My lovesickness you must see
accepts no other cure
than healing from your presence and figure.

O crystalline sparkling brook,
if on your silvery face it could transpire
to suddenly form the look
of the eyes I desire
that deep within my heart are sketched in fire!

Love, make those eyes depart,
for I am taking flight!
    (Bridegroom)
— Return my dove,
for now the wounded hart
is on the hill above
refreshed by breezes from your flight of love!
    (Bride)
My Love, the mountain heights,
the wooded vales where solitude is found,
the islands' singular sights,
the rivers' pleasing sound,
the whistling loving breezes that abound,

la noche sosegada
en par de los levantes de la aurora,
la música callada,
la soledad sonora,
la cena que recrea y enamora.

Cazadnos las raposas,
que está ya florecida nuestra viña,
en tanto que de rosas
hacemos una piña,
y no parezca nadie en la montiña.

Detente, cierzo muerto;
ven, austro, que recuerdas los amores,
aspira por mi huerto,
y corran sus olores,
y pacerá el Amado entre las flores.

¡Oh ninfas de Judea!
en tanto que en las flores y rosales
y ámbar perfumea,
morá en los arrabales,
y no queráis tocar nuestros umbrales.

Escóndete, Carillo,
y mira con tu haz a las montañas,
y no quieras decillo;
mas mira las compañas
de la que va por ínsulas extrañas.

the night of peaceful calm
before the east winds' rise at break of day,
the silent music's balm,
the solitude's sonorous way,
the supper that delights with lovers' play.

All foxes keep away,
our vineyard is now blossoming on its own;
with roses we'll display
our making a pine cone,
let none appear upon the hill alone.

Be still north wind of death;
come, south wind's memory of love's warm glow,
and let your fragrant breath
throughout my garden flow,
and grazing in the flowers my Love will go.

You young Judean girls,
while in the flowers and roses we adore
the amber perfume swirls,
stay far off I implore,
seek not to touch our thresholds evermore.

Now hide from view, my Dear,
and turn your face to gaze at mountain heights,
no speaking let us hear,
but see all the delights
of her who goes for islands singular sights.

(Esposo)
A las aves ligeras,
leones, ciervos, gamos saltadores,
montes, valles, riberas,
aguas, aires, ardores,
y miedos de las noches veladores:

por las amenas liras
y canto de serenas os conjuro
que cesen vuestras iras,
y no toqués al muro,
porque la esposa duerma más seguro.

Entrado se ha la esposa
en el ameno huerto deseado,
y a su sabor reposa,
el cuello reclinado
sobre los dulces brazos del Amado.

Debajo del manzano,
allí conmigo fuiste desposada;
allí te di la mano
y fuiste reparada
donde tu madre fuera violada.

(Esposa)
Nuestro lecho florido,
de cuevas de leones enlazado,
en púrpura tendido,
de paz edificado,
de mil escudos de oro coronado.

(Bridegroom)
To birds that swiftly soar,
stags, lions, leaping bucks of fallow deer,
mounts, valleys, river shore,
winds, waters, heat to sear,
and worries of the watchful nights of fear:

by the delightful lyre
and siren's singing, all you I conjure
to cease to feel your ire,
your touch no wall endure,
so that the bride may sleep in peace secure.

Within the bride now goes
into the pleasant garden of her desires,
contented in repose,
her neck drops, she retires
on his sweet arms who all this love inspires.

Beneath the apple tree,
you came to me, our marriage did begin;
I gave my hand to see
you were redeemed again,
where once your mother was defiled by sin.
(Bride)
Our bed is now in flower,
secured around by dens of lions bold,
a purple covered bower,
edified by peace untold,
and crowning it a thousand shields of gold.

A zaga de tu huella
las jóvenes discurren al camino,
al toque de centella,
al adobado vino,
emisiones de bálsamo divino.

En la interior bodega
de mi Amado bebí, y cuando salía
por toda aquesta vega,
ya cosa no sabía;
y el ganado perdí que antes seguía.

Allí me dio su pecho,
allí me enseñó ciencia muy sabrosa;
y yo le di de hecho
a mí, sin dejar cosa;
allí le prometí de ser su esposa.

Mi alma se ha empleado,
y todo mi caudal en su servicio;
ya no guardo ganado,
ni ya tengo otro oficio,
que ya sólo en amar es mi ejercicio.

Pues ya si en el ejido
de hoy más no fuere vista ni hallada,
diréis que me ha perdido;
que, andando enamorada,
me hice perdidiza y fui ganada.

Behind your footprints' mark
along the road go maidens to and fro,
a touch of inner spark,
the spiced wine's heady glow,
love's outpourings from balm divine now flow.

In wine vaults deep below
I drank of my Beloved; going out
through all of this meadow,
no thing I knew about;
the herd I followed lost, I went without.

There he gave me his breast,
and taught me a delightful way of knowing;
I gave to him the rest
of me, held back no thing;
and promised him to be his bride ongoing.

All mine I now expend
to serve his will, my soul and all I own;
the herd I no more tend,
all other work disown,
my only occupation, love alone.

If I am no more seen
nor found to go upon the common ground,
you will say lost I've been;
that, wandering by love bound,
I made myself be lost and then was found.

De flores y esmeraldas,
en las frescas mañanas escogidas,
haremos las guirnaldas
en tu amor florecidas
y en un cabello mío entretejidas.

En solo aquel cabello
que en mi cuello volar consideraste,
mirástele en mi cuello,
y en él preso quedaste,
y en uno de mis ojos te llagaste.

Cuando tú me mirabas
su gracia en mí tus ojos imprimían;
por eso me adamabas,
y en eso merecían
los míos adorar lo que en ti vían.

No quieras despreciarme,
que, si color moreno en mí hallaste,
ya bien puedes mirarme
después que me miraste,
que gracia y hermosura en mí dejaste.

    (Esposo)
La blanca palomica
al arca con el ramo se ha tornado;
y ya la tortolica
al socio deseado
en las riberas verdes ha hallado.

With flowers and emeralds rare,
collected in the cool of morning sunshine,
the garlands we prepare,
that flower in love divine,
are bound with one hair from this head of mine.

Alone that single hair,
that on my neck was flying in your view,
you saw on my neck there,
it captivated you,
and one of my eyes left you wounded too.

When your gaze fell upon me
your eyes caused grace within me deep to burn;
for this you loved me strongly,
and thus my eyes return
adoring love that in you they discern.

Do not your love despise
if darkness colored all in me you found,
now you may feast your eyes
on me, since your looks crowned
with grace and beauty, given till they abound.
    (Bridegroom)
And so the small white dove,
with branch in grasp back to the ark retired;
and now the turtledove
has found, by love inspired,
on the green river banks the mate desired.

En soledad vivía,
y en soledad ha puesto ya su nido,
y en soledad la guía
a solas su querido,
también en soledad de amor herido.

(*Esposa*)
Gocémonos, Amado,
y vámonos a ver en tu hermosura
al monte y al collado
do mana el agua pura;
entremos más adentro en la espesura,

y luego a las subidas
cavernas de la piedra nos iremos,
que están bien escondidas,
y allí nos entraremos,
y el mosto de granadas gustaremos.

Allí me mostrarías
aquello que mi alma pretendía,
y luego me darías
allí, tú, ¡vida mía!
aquello que me diste el otro día:

el aspirar del aire,
el canto de la dulce filomena,
el soto y su donaire,
en la noche serena,
con llama que consume y no da pena.

Que nadie lo miraba;
Aminidab tampoco parecía
y el cerco sosegaba
y la caballería
a vista de las aguas descendía.

In solitude she bided,
in solitude she now has built her nest,
in solitude he guided
her lone on lover's quest,
he too in solitude by love's wound blest.

(Bride)
Let us rejoice, my Love;
to see us in your beauty let us go
to mount and hill above,
where the pure waters flow;
and deep into the thicket more to know,

and then we scale the height,
up to the caverns in the rock, so placed
they are well hid from sight,
and entering in haste,
the juice of pomegranates we will taste.

To me there you will show
the things my soul has sought for to enshrine;
on me you will bestow
there, you, this life of mine!
what you gave me that other day divine:

the breathing of the air,
the nightingale that sings its sweet refrain,
the grove so gracefully fair,
in the serene night's reign,
with flame consuming and that gives no pain.

She was where none could see;
appearance of Aminidab now ended;
the siege raised peacefully,
the cavalry suspended,
at sighting of the waters, now descended.

Sin Arrimo y Con Arrimo

Sin arrimo y con arrimo,
sin luz y a oscuras viviendo,
todo me voy consumiendo.

Mi alma está desasida
de toda cosa criada,
y sobre sí levantada,
y en una sabrosa vida
sólo en su Dios arrimada.
Por eso ya se dirá
la cosa que más estimo,
que mi alma se ve ya
sin arrimo y con arrimo.

Y, aunque tinieblas padezco
en esta vida mortal,
no es tan crecido mi mal,
porque, si de luz carezco,
tengo vida celestial;
porque el amor de tal vida,
cuando más ciego va siendo,
que tiene al alma rendida,
sin luz y a oscuras viviendo.

Unsupported and Supported

Unsupported and supported,
living lacking light of day,
I am wholly burned away.

Free — my soul now loosed in flight
from all things that are created,
o'er itself is elevated,
in a life of pure delight,
just by God's support elated.
For all that it can be said
I most value how transported
my soul sees itself, now led
unsupported and supported.

Though I suffer a dark night
in this life of mortal bane,
that brings no o'erwhelming pain,
even if I lack the light,
I have heavenly life to gain;
for this life the love so tender,
when more blind becomes my way,
holds the soul in sweet surrender,
living lacking light of day,

Hace tal obra el amor
después que le conocí,
que, si hay bien o mal en mí,
todo lo hace de un sabor,
y al alma transforma en sí;
y así, en su llama sabrosa,
la cual en mí estoy sintiendo,
apriesa, sin quedar cosa,
todo me voy consumiendo.

Love performs in such a measure,
when one comes to know its spell,
all things good and bad that dwell
in me are all turned to pleasure,
and the soul transformed as well;
so, in its delightful flame,
felt within me as I pray,
swiftly, naught to stay the same,
I am wholly burned away.

Entréme Donde No Supe

Entréme donde no supe,
y quedéme no sabiendo,
toda ciencia trascendiendo.

Yo no supe dónde estaba,
pero, cuando allí me vi,
sin saber dónde me estaba,
grandes cosas entendí;
no diré lo que sentí,
que me quedé no sabiendo,
toda ciencia trascendiendo.

De paz y de piedad
era la ciencia perfecta,
en profunda soledad
entendida, vía recta;
era cosa tan secreta,
que me quedé balbuciendo,
toda ciencia trascendiendo.

Entering A Place Unknown

Entering a place unknown
made unknowing be my ending,
all my knowledge there transcending.

Knowing not just where I was,
when I there myself could see,
without knowing where I was,
greatest learning came to me;
what I felt, a mystery,
but unknowing was my ending,
all my knowledge there transcending.

All of piety and peace
in that perfect knowledge lay;
in deep solitude's release
I now knew the narrow way;
such a secret way to pray
left me stammering at the ending,
all my knowledge far transcending.

Estaba tan embebido,
tan absorto y ajenado,
que se quedó mi sentido
de todo sentir privado,
y el espíritu dotado
de un entender no entendiendo,
toda ciencia trascendiendo.

El que allí llega de vero
de sí mismo desfallece;
cuanto sabía primero
mucho bajo le parece,
y su ciencia tanto crece,
que se queda no sabiendo,
toda ciencia trascendiendo.

Cuanto más alto se sube,
tanto menos se entendía,
que es la tenebrosa nube
que a la noche esclarecía;
por eso quien la sabía
queda siempre no sabiendo,
toda ciencia trascendiendo.

Este saber no sabiendo
es de tan alto poder,
que los sabios arguyendo
jamás le pueden vencer;
que no llega su saber
a no entender entendiendo,
toda ciencia trascendiendo.

I was ravished and bereft,
so absorbed and inward driven,
that my senses were all left
from my feelings fully riven,
and my spirit freely given
to unknowing's comprehending,
all my knowledge far transcending.

He who comes there, it is true,
will soon find himself grow weak,
everything he thought he knew
seems too commonplace to speak,
as his knowledge grows he'll seek
in unknowing for his ending,
all his knowledge there transcending.

How e'er higher he ascends,
more obscure is his insight,
'tis the darkest cloud he rends
that illuminates the night;
so the one who sees this light
in unknowing seeks his ending,
all his knowledge there transcending.

This same knowledge in unknowing
is of such enormous power,
that all wise disputers' showing
of their learning can't empower
them to ever scale the tower
to unknowing's comprehending,
all their knowledge there transcending.

Y es de tan alta excelencia
aqueste sumo saber,
que no hay facultad ni ciencia
que le puedan emprender
quien se supiere vencer
con un no saber sabiendo,
irá siempre trascendiendo.

Y, si lo queréis oír,
consiste esta suma ciencia
es un subido sentir
de la divinal esencia;
es obra de su clemencia
hacer quedar no entendiendo,
toda ciencia trascendiendo.

And it is of such great worth,
this exalted form of knowing,
power and learning of this earth
ne'er attain it without showing
mastery of self ongoing,
with unknowing's comprehending
always going on transcending.

And if you should wish to know,
this high knowledge where to mine,
seek that finest feeling's glow
from the essence of divine
mercy, working to refine
us, unknowing as our ending,
all our knowledge now transcending.

Sino Por Un No Sé Qué

Por toda la hermosura
nunca yo me perderé
sino por un no sé qué
que se alcanza por ventura.

Sabor de bien que es finito,
lo más que puede llegar
es cansar el apetito
y estragar el paladar;
y así, por toda dulzura
nunca yo me perderé,
sino por un no sé qué
que se halla por ventura.

El corazón generoso
nunca cura de parar
donde se puede pasar,
sino en más dificultoso;
nada le causa hartura,
y sube tanto su fe,
que gusta de un no sé qué
que se halla por ventura.

Only For A Know-Not-What

For all beauty that is known
never would I lose my lot,
only for a know-not-what
that is gained through grace alone.

Savoring goods that are finite
only brings to life more toil,
wearing out the appetite,
and the palate sure to spoil;
so for all the sweetness known
never would I lose my lot,
only for a know-not-what
that is found through grace alone.

Never will the generous heart
tolerate the least delay
where'er it can find a way,
though it be the hardest part;
naught that satisfies is known,
faith ascending as it ought,
tasting of a know-not-what
that is found through grace alone.

El que de amor adolece,
del divino ser tocado,
tiene el gusto tan trocado
que a los gustos desfallece;
como el que con calentura
fastidia el manjar que ve,
y apetece un no sé qué
que se halla por ventura.

No os maravilléis de aquesto,
que el gusto se quede tal,
porque es la causa del mal
ajena de todo el resto;
y así toda criatura
enajenada se ve
y gusta de un no sé qué
que se halla por ventura.

Que estando la voluntad
de Divinidad tocada,
no puede quedar pagada
sino con Divinidad;
mas, por ser tal su hermosura
que sólo se ve por fe,
gústala un no sé qué
que se halla por ventura.

Pues, de tal enamorado,
decidme si habréis dolor,
pues que no tiene sabor
entre todo lo criado;
solo, sin forma y figura,
sin hallar arrimo y pie,
gustando allá un no sé qué
que se halla por ventura.

People by this love afflicted,
by the touch divine deranged,
find their taste have been so changed
what once pleased them is restricted;
as with fever fully blown
loathing food seen in a pot,
craving only know-not-what
that is found through grace alone.

Do not marvel at this more,
that the taste should stay this way,
for this sickness makes one pay
price far greater than before;
from all creatures one has known
now withdrawing from the lot,
tasting only know-not-what
that is found through grace alone.

Wills that know sublimity
by the touch of God's release,
can no longer find their peace
save with the Divinity;
more, this beauty will be shown,
without faith we know it not,
tasted in a know-not-what
that is found through grace alone.

With such love, then, giving birth,
tell me would you feel the pain,
of one with no joy to gain
in all creatures of this earth;
lone and lacking flesh or bone,
with support or foothold naught,
tasting there a know-not-what
that is found through grace alone.

No penséis que el interior,
que es de mucha más valía,
halla gozo y alegría
en lo que acá da sabor;
mas sobre toda hermosura,
y lo que es y será y fue,
gusta de allá un no sé qué
que se halla por ventura.

Más emplea su cuidado,
quien se quiere aventajar,
en lo que está por ganar
que en lo que tiene ganado;
y así, para más altura,
yo siempre me inclinaré
sobre todo a un no sé qué
que se halla por ventura.

Por lo que por el sentido
puede acá comprehenderse
y todo lo que entenderse,
aunque sea muy subido,
ni por gracia y hermosura
yo nunca me perderé,
sino por un no sé qué
que se halla por ventura.

Think not that the inner light,
that is of such greater worth,
makes one find pleasure and mirth
in all things that bring delight;
far beyond all beauty known,
what is, will be, was begot,
one tastes there a know-not-what
that is found through grace alone.

One must have a strong intent,
who wants always to progress,
to seek gain accomplished less
more than gain where competent;
so, to reach the highest throne,
I will always bend my thought
o'er all to a know-not-what
that is found through grace alone.

Not for things of which my sense
comprehends here on this earth
nor all knowledge and its worth,
though it highly recompense,
nor for grace and beauty known
never would I lose my lot,
only for a know-not-what
that is found through grace alone.

Tras De Un Amoroso Lance

Tras de un amoroso lance,
y no de esperanza falto,
volé tan alto, tan alto,
que le di a la caza alcance.

Para que yo alcance diese
a aqueste lance divino,
tanto volar me convino
que de vista me perdiese;
y, con todo, en este trance
en el vuelo quedé falto;
mas el amor fue tan alto,
que le di a la caza alcance.

Cuanto más alto subía
deslumbróseme la vista,
y la más fuerte conquista
en oscuro se hacía;
mas, por ser de amor el lance,
di un ciego y oscuro salto,
y fui tan alto, tan alto,
que le di a la caza alcance.

I Went In Pursuit By Love's Way

I went in pursuit by love's way;
my hope did not fail in the try,
I flew very high, oh so high,
at last overtaking the prey.

In order to gain me the right
to divine opportunity,
I flew high toward unity
and soon became lost out of sight;
with all, in this dangerous way
I faltered in my strength to fly,
yet love bore me ever more high,
at last overtaking the prey.

While rising so near to the light,
my vision was dazed by the glare,
and my greatest conquest was there
in darkest obscureness of night;
but since I was seeking love's way,
I blindly leapt in the dark sky,
and I flew so high, oh so high,
at last overtaking the prey.

Cuanto más alto llegaba
de este lance tan subido,
tanto más bajo y rendido
y abatido me hallaba;
dije: ¡No habrá quien alcance!;
y abatíme tanto, tanto,
que fui tan alto, tan alto,
que le di a la caza alcance.

Por una extraña manera
mil vuelos pasé de un vuelo,
porque esperanza del cielo
tanto alcanza cuanto espera;
esperé solo este lance,
y en esperar no fui falto,
pues fui tan alto, tan alto,
que le di a la caza alcance.

The higher became my ascent
within this search so excellent,
the lower became my descent
fatigued and o'erwhelmed, I was spent;
None can overtake! I would say;
it humbled and made me so dry,
that I flew so high, oh so high,
at last overtaking the prey.

By this rare endeavor to cope
one flight did a thousand excel,
for hope within heaven to dwell
gains fully the height of its hope;
I hoped just to search in this way,
my hope did not fail in the try,
since I flew so high, oh so high,
at last overtaking the prey.

Un Pastorcico

Un pastorcico solo está penado,
ajeno de placer y de contento,
y en su pastora puesto el pensamiento,
y el pecho del amor muy lastimado.

No llora por haberle amor llagado,
que no le pena verse así afligido,
aunque en el corazón está herido;
mas llora por pensar que está olvidado.

Que sólo de pensar que está olvidado
de su bella pastora, con gran pena
se deja maltratar in tierra ajena,
el pecho del amor muy lastimado.

Y dice el pastorcico: ¡Ay, desdichado
de aquel que de mi amor ha hecho ausencia
y no quiere gozar la mi presencia,
y el pecho por su amor muy lastimado!

Y a cabo de un gran rato se ha encumbrado
sobre un árbol, do abrió sus brazos bellos,
y muerto se ha quedado asido dellos,
el pecho del amor muy lastimado.

A Lone Young Shepherd

A lone young shepherd lives in pain apart
from all that pleases and that makes content;
fixed on his shepherdess his sentiment,
his love has caused a deep wound in his heart.

He weeps not from the wound love has begotten,
affliction like this does not cause him pain,
although his heart deep injury did sustain;
he weeps more from the thought he's been forgotten.

The thought that he's forgotten on the part
of his fair shepherdess gives great pain, and
he yields to be abused in foreign land,
his love has caused a deep wound in his heart.

The shepherd says: Ay, wretch that she depart,
her portion of my love now but its absence,
and does not seek enjoyment of my presence,
though love for her did sorely wound my heart.

Then after a long time his climb did start
to tree top, where his lovely arms he spread,
and hanging by them stayed till he was dead,
his love has caused a deep wound in his heart.

Vivo Sin Vivir En Mí

Vivo sin vivir en mí
y de tal manera espero,
que muero porque no muero.

En mí yo no vivo ya,
y sin Dios vivir no puedo;
pues sin él y sin mí quedo,
este vivir ¿qué será?
Mil muertes se me hará,
pues mi misma vida espero,
muriendo porque no muero.

Esta vida que yo vivo
es privación de vivir;
y así, es continuo morir
hasta que viva contigo.
Oye, mi Dios, lo que digo;
que esta vida no la quiero,
que muero porque no muero.

I Live Lacking Life In Me

I live lacking life in me,
and my hope is such I sigh,
that I die since I don't die.

I no longer live in me,
without God all life is vain;
without him what will remain
of this life, what will it be?
Thousand deaths in agony,
as I watch my life pass by,
and I die since I don't die.

This life that I live today
is privation now to live;
constant death to me does give
till I live with you, I pray:
Listen, God, to what I say;
no more love for life have I,
and I die since I don't die.

Estando ausente de ti
¿qué vida puedo tener,
sino muerte padecer
la mayor que nunca vi?
Lástima tengo de mí,
pues de suerte persevero,
que muero porque no muero.

El pez que del agua sale
aun de alivio no carece,
que en la muerte que padece
al fin la muerte le vale.
¿Qué muerte habrá que se iguale
a mi vivir lastimero,
pues si más vivo más muero?

Cuando me pienso aliviar
de verte en el Sacramento,
háceme más sentimiento
el no te poder gozar;
todo es para más penar
por no verte como quiero,
y muero porque no muero.

Y si me gozo, Señor,
con esperanza de verte,
en ver que puedo perderte
se me dobla mi dolor;
viviendo en tanto pavor
y esperando como espero,
muérome porque no muero.

Being so removed from you
what of life can I secure,
but the death I must endure,
very worst I ever knew?
How I pity me 'tis true,
since my fate is life, I cry
that I die since I don't die.

Fish that's taken from the sea
does not lack this consolation,
that its dying suffocation
in the end by death sets free.
Oh what death could equal be
to my life of grief, since I
living more, will e'er more die?

When I think to ease the strain
with you in the Sacrament,
it makes worse my discontent
to be lacking you again;
now all things add to my pain
not to see you though I try,
and I die since I don't die.

And if I rejoice, my Lord,
in the hope of seeing you,
I see I can lose you too
doubling my sad discord;
I live fearing lost reward,
yet I hope as time goes by,
and I die since I don't die.

¡Sácame de aquesta muerte,
mi Dios, y dame la vida;
no me tengas impedida
en este lazo tan fuerte;
mira que peno por verte,
y mi mal es tan entero,
que muero porque no muero!

Lloraré me muerte ya
y lamentaré mi vida,
en tanto que detenida
por mis pecados está.
¡Oh mi Dios!, ¿cuando será
cuando yo diga de vero:
vivo ya porque no muero?

From this death deliver me,
oh my God, and give me life,
don't constrain me, take your knife;
from these bonds now cut me free;
how I suffer, you to see,
and my hurt so deep I cry,
that I die since I don't die!

I will mourn the death of me,
and lament my life of pain,
for as long as I remain
for my sins apart from thee.
Oh my God!, when will it be
when I can say without lie:
I live now since I don't die?

Romance sobre el salmo
"Super Flumina Babilonis"

Encima de las corrientes
que en Babilonia hallaba,
allí me senté llorando,
allí la tierra regaba,

acordándome de ti,
¡oh Sión!, a quien amaba.
Era dulce tu memoria,
y con ella más lloraba.

Dejé los trajes de fiesta,
los de trabajo tomaba,
y colgué en los verdes sauces
la música que llevaba,

poneiéndola en esperanza
de aquello que en ti esperaba.
Allí me hirió el amor,
y el corazón me sacaba.

Díjele que me matase,
pues de tal suerte llagaba:
yo me metía en su fuego,
sabiendo que me abrasaba,

Romance On The Psalm
"By The Waters Of Babylon"

Alongside the flowing waters
that in Babylon are found,
there I sat myself down weeping,
my tears watering the ground,

to recall the memory of you,
Zion! whom I so adore.
'Twas the sweetest memory, and
with it weeping came the more.

I removed my festive clothing,
working garments to be worn,
and I hung on the green willows
all the music I had borne,

placed it there in hope of what I
hoped for from you at the start.
I was wounded by a love which
dispossessed me of my heart.

I had asked that love would kill me,
since its wound was so severe;
threw myself into its fire, then,
knowing how the flames would sear,

disculpando el avecica
que en el fuego se acababa.
Estábame en mí muriendo,
y en ti sólo respiraba,

en mí por ti me moría
y por ti resucitaba,
que la memoria de ti
daba vida y la quitaba.

Gozábanse los extraños
entre quien cautivo estaba;
preguntábanme cantares
de lo que en Sión cantaba:
— Canta de Sión un himno,
veamos cómo sonaba.

— Decid: ¿Cómo en tierra ajena,
donde por Sión lloraba,
cantaré yo la alegría
que en Sión se me quedaba?
Echaríala en olvido
si en la ajena me gozaba.

Con mi paladar se junte
la lengua con que hablaba,
si de ti yo me olvidare,
en la tierra do moraba.

¡Sión, por los verdes ramos
que Babilonia me daba,
de mí se olvide mi diestra,
que es lo que en ti más amaba,

and excusing the young bird that
in the fire would meet its death.
I within myself was dying,
in you only taking breath,

in me for you I was dying,
for you I revived again,
for by memory of you one
does both lose life and regain.

They were glad, the strangers midst whom
in captivity I was bound;
asking me to sing songs for them
that in Zion can be found:
Sing the hymns for us of Zion,
let us now hear how they sound.

I said: How in foreign land where
just for Zion do I cry,
could I sing of all the joy I
knew in Zion days gone by?
I would be forgetting her if
I rejoiced neath foreign sky.

May my palate join my tongue and
all my speaking end as well,
if I ever should forget you
in the land where I must dwell.

Zion, by the branches green which
Babylon has given me,
may my right hand be forgotten,
though loved most in liberty,

si de ti no me acordare,
en lo que más me gozaba,
y si yo tuviese fiesta,
y sin ti la festejaba!

¡Oh hija de Babilonia,
mísera y desventurada!
Bienaventurado era
aquel en quien confiaba,
que te ha de dar el castigo
que de tu mano llevaba,

y juntará sus pequeños,
y a mí, porque en ti lloraba,
a la piedra, que era Cristo,
por el cual yo te dejaba.

if I don't remember you, who
gave to me the greatest glee,
or I have a single feast, or
without you festivity!

Babylon, your daughter wretched
and so full of misery!
May the one whom I have trusted
evermore so blessed be,
and to you give punishment that
your hand gave so onerously,

he will gather all his small ones
you made weep, including me,
at the rock who is the Christ, for
whom I left you to be free.

Que Bien Sé Yo La Fonte

Que bien sé yo la fonte que mana y corre,
aunque es de noche.

Aquella eterna fonte está escondida,
que bien sé yo do tiene su manida,
aunque es de noche.

Su origen no lo sé, pues no le tiene,
mas sé que todo origen de ella viene,
aunque es de noche.

Sé que no puede ser cosa tan bella,
y que cielos y tierra beben de ella,
aunque es de noche.

Bien sé que suelo en ella no se halla,
y que ninguno puede vadealla,
aunque es de noche.

Su claridad nunca es oscurecida,
y sé que toda luz de ella es venida,
aunque es de noche.

Sé ser tan caudalosos sus corrientes,
que infiernos, cielos riegan y las gentes,
aunque es de noche.

For Well I Know The Spring

For well I know the spring that flows so free,
although it is night.

That fountain is eternal and concealed,
though well I know from where it is revealed,
although it is night.

Its origin, unknown, nor has it one,
yet from her have all origins begun,
although it is night.

I know there can't be any thing so fair,
and that the heavens and earth both drink from there,
although it is night.

I know no one its bottom e'er could sound,
no way to cross it ever could be found,
although it is night.

Its clarity ne'er is made to be obscure,
I know each ray of light has come from her,
although it is night.

I know that it's so full its currents swell,
and water all the people, heaven and hell,
although it is night.

El corriente que nace de esta fuente
bien sé que es tan capaz y omnipotente,
aunque es de noche.

El corriente que de estas dos procede
sé que ninguna de ellas le precede,
aunque es de noche.

Aquesta eterna fonte está escondida
en este vivo pan por darnos vida,
aunque es de noche.

Aquí está llamando a las criaturas,
y de esta agua se hartan, aunque a oscuras,
porque es de noche.

Aquesta viva fuente que deseo,
en este pan de vida yo la veo,
aunque es de noche.

The stream that's born with this spring as its source,
I know is such a broad and powerful force,
although it is night.

The stream which from these other two proceeds
I know that neither of the two precedes,
although it is night.

This fount eternal is so well concealed
in living bread that to us life does yield,
although it is night.

Here it is, calling out to each creature,
this water quenches thirst, although obscure,
because it is night.

This living spring which I desire in me,
within this bread of life I now can see,
although it is night.

Romances

1. *Romance sobre el Evangelio*
"In principio erat Verbum,"
acerca de la Santisima Trinidad.

En el principio moraba
el Verbo, y en Dios vivía,
en quien su felicidad
infinita poseía.

El mismo Verbo Dios era,
que el principio se decía;
él moraba en el principio,
y principio no tenía.

El era el mismo principio,
por eso de él carecía.
El Verbo se llama Hijo,
que del principio nacía;

hale siempre concebido
y siempre le concebía;
dale siempre su sustancia,
y siempre se la tenía.

Y así la gloria del Hijo
es la que en el Padre había,
y toda su gloria el Padre
en el Hijo poseía.

Romances

1. *Romance on the Gospel*
   "In the beginning was the Word,"
   regarding the Blessed Trinity.

At beginning of creation
was the Word, within God living,
in whom boundless happiness his
life in God to him was giving.

That same Word was God himself, whom
the beginning was said to be;
he exists from the beginning,
no beginning e'er had he.

He himself was the beginning,
only for him was there need.
The Word, also called the Son, was
of beginning born indeed;

He has always been conceived and
is forever being conceived;
giving always of his substance,
which is always being received.

Thus the glory of the Son and
of the Father are as one,
and the Father now possesses
all his glory in the Son.

Como amado en el amante
uno en otro residía,
y aquese amor que los une
en lo mismo convenía

con el uno y con el otro
en igualdad y valía.
Tres Personas y un amado
entre todos tres había,

y un amor en todas ellas
y un amante las hacía,
y el amante es el amado
en que cada cual vivía;

que el ser que los tres poseen
cada cual le poseía,
y cada cual de ellos ama
a la que este ser tenía.

Este ser es cada una,
y éste solo las unía
en un inefable nudo
que decir no se sabía;

por lo cual era infinito
el amor que las unía,
porque un solo amor tres tienen,
que su esencia se decía;
que el amor cuanto más uno,
tanto más amor hacía.

As with lover in beloved
each within the other resides,
and this love that joins together
in each of them coincides

with the one and with the other
in equality and worth.
Just three Persons, one beloved,
and among all three no dearth,

and one love in all of them makes
them one lover who does give,
and the lover is beloved
in whom each of them does live;

for the being shared by these three
every one of them possesses,
and each one of them is loving
each one whom this being blesses.

Each one of them is this being,
union comes from this alone,
in a knot ineffable that
is beyond words, and unknown;

for this reason it is boundless
love, which is their union,
for the three have just one love which
is their essence, said and done;
and that love grows ever greater
as it grows more into one.

2. *De la comunicación de las tres Personas.*

En aquel amor inmenso
que de los dos procedía,
palabras de gran regalo
el Padre al Hijo decía,

de tan profundo deleite,
que nadie las entendía;
sólo el Hijo lo gozaba,
que es a quien pertenecía.

Pero aquello que se entiende,
de esta manera decía:
"Nada me contenta, Hijo,
fuera de tu compañía;

y si algo me contenta,
en ti mismo lo quería.
El que a ti más se parece
a mí más satisfacía,

y el que en nada te semeja
en mí nada hallaría.
En ti solo me he agradado,
¡oh vida de vida mía!

Eres lumbre de mi lumbre,
eres mi sabiduría,
figura de mi sustancia,
en quien bien me complacía.

2. *On the communication*
   of the three Persons.

In immensity of love that
from the two of them had come,
words of great gratification
spoke the Father to the Son,

with profoundness of delight that
no one e'er could understand;
for the Son alone rejoiced, since
it was for him they were planned.

That which could be comprehended
of these words was said to be:
"No thing pleases me, my Son, but
to be in your company;

and if some thing pleases me, in
you yourself I love that thing.
He who most resembles you, my
satisfaction most will bring,

he who is like you in nothing
will find naught in me to see.
In you only am I pleased, oh
life of the life that's in me!

You're the light that lights my splendor,
all my wisdom you have seized,
very image of my substance,
in whom I am so well pleased.

Al que a ti te amare, Hijo,
a mi mismo le daría,
y el amor que yo en ti tengo
ese mismo en él pondría,
el razón de haber amado
a quien yo tanto quería."

3. *De la creación.*

"Una esposa que te ame,
mi Hijo, darte quería,
que por tu valor merezca
tener nuestra compañía

y comer pan a una mesa,
del mismo que yo comía,
porque conozca los bienes
que en tal Hijo yo tenía,
y se congracie conmigo
de tu gracia y lozanía."

"Mucho lo agradezco, Padre,
— el Hijo le respondía — ;
a la esposa que me dieres
yo mi claridad daría,

para que por ella vea
cuánto mi Padre valía,
y cómo el ser que poseo
de su ser le recibía.

Reclinarla he yo en mi brazo,
y en tu amor se abrasaría,
y con eterno deleite
tu bondad sublimaría."

He who gives to you his love, Son,
I will give to him my grace,
and the love I bear for you now
in him also will I place,
for he loved the one whom my love
does so totally embrace."

3. *On the creation.*

"Son, it is my wish to give a
bride who'll treat you lovingly,
and because of your worth will be
worthy of our company,

and to eat at table the same
bread upon which I now dine,
so that she may know the good that
I have in this Son of mine,
and that she enjoy with me your
splendor and your grace divine."

"I am very grateful, Father,"
Son then answered in reply;
"to the bride that you give me I'll
show my glory from on high,

so that by it she may see how
great my Father truly is,
how the being I possess came
from the being that is his.

I'll lean her back on my arm, and
she will feel your love inflame,
with delight eternal she will
praise the goodness of your name."

4. *Prosigue*

"Hágase, pues — dijo el Padre — ,
que tu amor lo merecía";
y en este dicho que dijo,
el mundo criado había

palacio para la esposa
hecho en gran sabiduría;
el cual en dos aposentos,
alto y bajo, dividía.

El bajo de diferencias
infinitas componía;
mas el alto hermoseaba
de admirable pedrería,
porque conozca la esposa
el Esposo que tenía.

En el alto colocaba
la angélica jerarquía;
pero la natura humana
en el bajo la ponía,
por ser en su compostura
algo de menor valía.

Y aunque el ser y los lugares
de esta suerte los partía,
pero todos son un cuerpo
de la esposa que decía;
que el amor de un mismo Esposo
una esposa los hacía.

4. Continues

"Be it done, then," said the Father
"by your love deservedly";
just by uttering these words, the
world's creation came to be;

palace for the bride he built, which
in great wisdom was provided;
with two separate dwelling places,
high and low they were divided.

So the lower place was built with
infinite variety
while the higher, beautified with
jewels of finest quality,
that the bride might come to know the
Bridegroom's singularity.

In the higher one were placed the
hierarchy of angel;
but the humans were all given the
lower place in which to dwell,
for they are in composition
of less worth than the angel.

Though each being and all places
in this way he did divide,
yet all form a single body
of the one who's called the bride;
for the love of the same Bridegroom
made as one to coincide.

Los de arriba poseían
el Esposo en alegría;
los de abajo, en esperanza
de fe que les infundía,
diciéndoles que algún tiempo
él los engrandecería

y que aquella su bajeza
él se la levantaría
de manera que ninguno
ya la vituperaría;

porque en todo semejante
él a ellos se haría
y se vendría con ellos,
y con ellos moraría;

y que Dios sería hombre,
y que el hombre Dios sería,
y trataría con ellos,
comería y bebería;

y que con ellos contino
él mismo se quedaría,
hasta que se consumase
este siglo que corría,

cuando se gozaran juntos
en eterna melodía;
porque él era la cabeza
de la esposa que tenía

a la cual todos los miembros
de los justos juntaría,
que son cuerpo de la esposa,
a la cual él tomaría

Those above possessed the Bridegroom
in great joy and ecstasy;
those below in hope that rises
from the faith infused as he
said to them that at some time they
would with him exalted be

and that he would raise them up so
far above their lowly state
in a way that no one e'er would
them again vituperate;

he would make himself to be so
wholly like them them none could tell,
and come down to be among them,
and among them he would dwell;

and so God would come to be man,
also God this man would be,
he would eat and drink with them and
talk to them with intimacy;

and continually with them
he himself would ever stay,
till the final consummation
when this age had passed away,

when they would rejoice together
in eternal melody;
for he was the head of the bride
that he holds eternally

with whom each and every member
of the just would now unite,
that are body of the bride, whom
he would now take with delight

en sus brazos tiernamente,
y allí su amor la daría;
y que, así juntos en uno,
al Padre la llevaría,

donde del mismo deleite
que Dios goza, gozaría;
que, como el Padre y el Hijo,
y el que de ellos procedía

el uno vive en el otro,
así la esposa sería,
que, dentro de Dios absorta,
vida de Dios viviría.

5. *Prosigue*

Con esta buena esperanza
que de arriba les venía,
el tedio de sus trabajos
más leve se les hacía;

pero la esperanza larga
y el deseo que crecía
de gozarse con su Esposo
contino les afligía;

por lo cual con oraciones,
con suspiros y agonía,
con lágrimas y gemidos
le rogaban noche y día
que ya se determinase
a les dar su compañía.

in his arms so tenderly, and
there would give to her his love;
when they were thus joined as one, would
lift her to the Father above,

where the very same delight that
God enjoys is hers indeed;
for as Father and the Son, and
he who from them does proceed

each one living in the other,
to the bride this gift they'll give,
taken wholly into God, the
life of God is what she'll live.

5. *Continues*

With the goodness of this hope which
to them from above had come,
all the tedium of their labors
was now lightened for them some;

but as hope was long delayed and
their desire would ever grow
for rejoicing with their Bridegroom
constant torment they would know;

so with prayerful intercessions,
and with sighs and agony,
with such tearfulness and groanings
night and day they made this plea
that he would at once determine
to give them his company.

Unos decían: "¡O si fuese
en mi tiempo el alegría!"
Otros: "¡Acaba, Señor;
al que has de enviar, envía!"

Otros: "¡O si ya rompieses
esos cielos, y vería
con mis ojos que bajases,
y mi llanto cesaría!"

"¡Regad, nubes de lo alto,
que la tierra lo pedía
y ábrase ya la tierra,
que espinas nos producía,
y produzca aquella flor
con que ella florecería!"

Otros decían: "¡Oh dichoso
el que en tal tiempo sería,
que merezca ver a Dios
con los ojos que tenía,

y tratarle con sus manos,
y andar en su compañía,
y gozar de los misterios
que entonces ordenaría!"

6. *Prosigue*

En aquestos y otros ruegos
gran tiempo pasado había;
pero en los postreros años
el fervor mucho crecía,

Some would say: "O, only if this
joy would come yet while I live!"
Others: "Now complete it, Lord;
give the one you have to give!"

Others: "O, if I could now see
with my eyes the heavens rend,
and behold him while descending,
then my tears at last would end!"

"Rain you down, clouds from on high, to
satisfy the earthly need,
and now let the earth be open
which gave us thorns from its seed,
and let it bring forth that flower
which its flowering is indeed!"

Others said: "O happiness for
him who at that time will be
still alive and fully able
with his own eyes God to see,

then to touch him with his hands, and
to walk in his company,
and enjoy what he ordains
sharing in his mystery!"

6. *Continues*

In these prayers and many others
a long time had passed away;
but in later years the fervor
grew much stronger day by day,

cuando el viejo Simeón
en deseo se encendía,
rogando a Dios que quisiese
dejalle ver este día.

Y así, el Espíritu Santo
al buen viejo respondía:
Que le daba su palabra
que la muerte no vería
hasta que la vida viese
que de arriba descendía,

y que él en sus mismas manos
al mismo Dios tomaría,
y le tendría en sus brazos
y consigo abrazaría

7. *Prosigue la Encarnación*

Ya que el tiempo era llegado
en que hacerse convenía
el rescate de la esposa,
que en duro yugo servía

debajo de aquella ley
que Moisés dado le había,
el Padre con amor tierno
de esta manera decía:

"Ya ves, Hijo, que a tu esposa
a tu imagen hecho había,
y en lo que a ti se parece
contigo bien convenía;

when the old man Simeon
with desire that burned would pray,
begging God he be allowed
to remain to see this day.

So it was, the Holy Spirit
answered with this guarantee,
promising the good old man that
his own death he would not see
till he saw the life descending
from that place so heavenly,

and within his very hands God
would indeed his own self place,
he would hold him in his arms then
keeping him in close embrace.

7. *Continues the Incarnation*

Now the time at last arrived when
it was deemed to be deserving
for the ransoming of the bride that
under hard yoke had been serving

underneath that very law that
Moses gave her to obey,
tenderly with love the Father
in this manner now did say:

"Son, you now see in your image
that your bride I did create,
in that she resembles you, she
will well suit you as your mate;

pero difiere en la carne
que en tu simple ser no había.
En los amores perfectos
esta ley se requería:

que se haga semejante
el amante a quien quería;
que la major semejanza
más deleite contenía;

el cual, sin duda, en tu esposa
grandemente crecería
si te viere semejante
en la carne que tenía."

Mi voluntad es la tuya
— el Hijo le respondía —
y la gloria que yo tengo
es tu voluntad ser mía,

y a mí me conviene, Padre,
lo que tu Alteza decía,
porque por esta manera
tu bondad más se vería;

veráse tu gran potencia,
justicia y sabiduría;
irélo a decir al mundo
y noticia le daría
de tu belleza y dulzura
y de tu soberanía.

but she's different in the flesh, of
which your simple being has naught.
In the love that's to be perfect
this law always must be taught:

that the lover to the loved one
in all ways must be alike,
for the greater is their likeness
greater will be their delight,

the delight your bride will feel would
doubtless very much have grown
if she were to see you like her
in the same flesh as her own."

"My will is for you alone", the
Son responded eagerly
"and all glory that I have is
that your will be done by me,

and to me it's fitting, Father,
all that you, the Most High, say;
for it is within this way you
will your goodness most display;

your great power and your justice
and your wisdom all will see;
I will go to tell the world now
spreading the word endlessly
of your beauty and your sweetness
and of all your sovereignty.

Iré a buscar a mi esposa,
y sobre mí tomaría
sus fatigas y trabajos,
en que tanto padecía;

y porque ella vida tenga,
yo por ella moriría,
y sacándola del lago
a ti te la volvería."

8. *Prosigue*

Entónces llamó a un arcángel
que san Gabriel se decía,
y enviólo a una doncella
que se llamaba María,

de cuyo consentimiento
el misterio se hacía;
en la cual la Trinidad
de carne al Verbo vestía;

y aunque tres hacen la obra,
en el uno se hacía;
y quedó el Verbo encarnado
en el vientre de María.

Y el que tenía sólo Padre,
ya también Madre tenía,
aunque no como cualquiera
que de varón concebía,

que de las entrañas de ella
él su carne recibía;
por lo cual Hijo de Dios
y del hombre se decía.

I will go to seek my bride, and
on myself will gladly bear
all her weariness and labors
which she suffers in despair;

and, so she may have life, I will
give my life for her and more,
rescuing her from the deep, to
you the bride I will restore."

8. *Continues*

Then he called on his archangel,
'twas Saint Gabriel by name,
to a virgin known as Mary
one night the archangel came;

with the virgin's free consent this
mystery was made to be,
that the Word was clothed in flesh
within her by the Trinity;

though the work was done by three, it
was completed in the one;
and the Word became incarnate,
within Mary's womb 'twas done.

He who only had a Father
now a mother had he too,
she was not like all the others
who conceive by men they knew,

from the essence of her being,
only her his flesh had grown;
for this reason Son of God and
son of man he now is known.

9. Del Nacimiento

Ya que era llegado el tiempo
en que de nacer había,
así como desposado
de su tálamo salía
abrazado con su esposa,
que en sus brazos la traía

al cual la graciosa Madre
en un pesebre ponía,
entre unos animales
que a la sazón allí había.

Los hombres decían cantares,
los ángeles melodía,
festejando el desposorio
que entre tales dos había.

Pero Dios en el pesebre
allí lloraba y gemía,
que eran joyas que la esposa
al desposorio traía.

Y la Madre estaba en pasmo
de que tal trueque veía:
el llanto del hombre en Dios,
y en el hombre la alegría,
lo cual del uno y del otro
tan ajeno se solía.

Finis

9. *On the Birth*

Now that season had arrived
when his birth was to take place,
like the bridegroom he came forth
from the bridal chamber's space
holding his bride in his arms,
clasping her in his embrace;

he whom graciously the Mother
did in manger gently place,
midst the various livestock that was
in there at that time of grace.

Men began to sing their songs, and
angels sang their melodies,
celebration of the marriage
joining lovers such as these.

But the infant God in manger
lying there now moaned and cried,
and these tears became the jewels brought
to the wedding by the bride.

And the Mother gazed in wonder
at this rare exchange to see:
weeping of the man in God, and
in the man was only glee,
which things to the one and other
were far passing strange to be.

Finish

Latrilla Navideña

Del Verbo divino
la Virgen preñada
viene de camino:
¡si le dais posada!

Christmas Refrain

Divine Word bestowed
in the Virgin's womb,
she comes down the road:
if you'll just make room!

Suma De La Perfección

Olvido de lo criado,
memoria del Criador,
atención a lo interior
y estarse amando al Amado.

Sum Of Perfection

Forgetting all things creaturely,
remembering the Creator,
attending to the interior,
and loving the One loving thee.

Santa Teresa de Jesús

(Saint Teresa of Avila)

Eficacia De La Paciencia

Nada te turbe,
nada te espante,
todo se pasa,
Dios no se muda,
la Paciencia
todo lo alcanza;
quien a Dios tiene
nada le falta.
Sólo Dios basta.

Efficacy Of Patience

Let nothing disturb you,
let nothing affright you,
for everything passes,
and God is unchanging,
through Patience
all things are obtained;
who holds fast to God
finds nothing is lacking.
God solely suffices.

Feliz El Que Ama a Dios

Dichoso el corazón enamorado
que en solo Dios ha puesto el pensamiento
por él renuncia todo lo criado,
y en él halla su gloria y su contento.
Aun de sí mismo vive descuidado,
porque en Dios está todo su intento
y así alegre pasa y muy gozoso
las ondas de este mar tempestuoso.

Happy The One Who Loves God

How happy the heart that by love is elated,
in which only God all its thought has embraced,
renouncing for him every thing that's created,
and finding its glory and joy by him graced.
Thus living with all thought of self so negated,
because in God all its intention is placed,
and so in great happiness and joyfully
it travels the waves of this turbulent sea.

Buscando A Dios

Alma, buscarte has en Mí,
y a Mí buscarme has en ti.

De tal suerte pudo amor,
alma, en mí te retratar,
que ningún sabio pintor
supiera con tal primor
tal imagen estampar.

Fuiste por amor criada
hermosa, bella, y así
en mis entrañas pintada,
si te perdieres, mi amada,
alma, buscarte has en Mí.

Que yo sé que te hallaras
en mi pecho retratada
y tan al vivo sacada
que si te ves te holgaras
viéndote tan bien pintada.

Y si acaso no supieres
donde me hallarás a Mí,
no andes de aquí para allí,
sino, si hallarme quiesieres
a Mí buscarme has en ti.

Seeking God

Soul, you must seek yourself in Me,
and in yourself you must seek Me.

Love was so able to portray,
dear soul, inside Me your likeness,
that no skilled painter could display
in such a lovely, artful way
your image formed with such finesse.

It was for love that you were made
with beauty, oh so perfectly,
within Me deep your form portrayed,
my love, if you are lost, dismayed,
soul, you must seek yourself in Me,

How well I know that you will find
yourself within my heart portrayed
so very lifelike there displayed
that seeing it will please your mind
to see a painting so well made.

And if perchance you do not know
where you must go for finding Me,
do not walk here or there to see,
but, if you wish to find Me, go
deep in yourself to seek for Me.

Porque tú eres me aposento,
eres mi casa y morada,
y así llamo en qualquier tiempo,
si hallo en tu pensamiento
estar la puerta cerrada.

Fuera de ti no hay buscarme,
porque para hallarme a Mí,
bastará solo llamarme,
que a ti iré sin tardarme
y a Mí buscarme has en ti.

Because you are this room of mine,
you are my house and dwelling place,
and thus I call at any time,
if in your thoughts I find that I'm
outside the door you closed to grace.

Do not seek Me so far away,
because to find Me it will be
enough my name alone to say,
to you I'll come without delay
and in yourself you must seek Me.

Coloquio Amoroso

Si el amor que me tenéis,
Dios mío, es como el que os tengo,
decidme ¿en qué me detengo?
O Vos ¿en qué os detenéis?

— Alma ¿qué quieres de mí?
— Dios mío, no más que verte.
— Y ¿qué temes más de ti?
— Lo que más temo es perderte.

Un alma en Dios escondida
¿qué tiene que desear,
sino amar y más amar,
y en amor toda escondida
tornarte de nuevo a amar?

Un amor que ocupe os pido,
Dios mío, mi alma os tenga,
para hacer un dulce nido
adonde más la convenga.

Loving Colloquy

If all the love you have for me,
my God, is like my love for you,
say, what detains me, that I do?
Or what is it delaying thee?

— Soul, what of me are your desires?
— My God, no more than you to see.
— And what most in you fear inspires?
— What I fear most is losing thee.

A soul within its God now hidden,
whatever else should it desire,
but to e'er greater love aspire,
and in that love remain all hidden,
returned anew into love's fire?

One love that owns me I request,
my God, my soul within you centered,
for making me the sweetest nest
where union can the best be entered.

Ante La Hermosura De Dios

¡Oh, Hermosura que excedéis
a todas las hermosuras!
Sin herir dolor hacéis
y sin dolor deshacéis,
el amor de las criaturas.

Oh, ñudo que así juntáis
dos cosas tan desiguales,
no sé por que os desatáis
pues atado fuerza dais
a tener por buen los males.

Quien no tiene ser juntáis
con el Ser que no se acaba;
sin acabar acabáis,
sin tener que amar amáis,
engrandecéis nuestra nada.

Before The Beauty Of God

Oh, what Beauty, you exceed
every other beauty's features!
Wounding not, you pained indeed,
without pain destroyed and freed
my love from all worldly creatures.

Oh, knot that so joins forever
two things as unlike as we,
unknown why our bond you sever,
since when tied you strengthen ever
and draw good from injury.

Bind that without being to
Being of eternity;
without finishing, now do,
not having to love, love too,
exalt our nonentity.

Sobre Aquellas Palabras "Dilectus Meus Mihi"

Yo toda me entregué y di,
y de tal suerte he trocado
que mi Amado para mí,
y yo soy para mí Amado.

Cuando el dulce Cazador
me tiró y dejó rendida,
en los brazos del amor,
mi alma quedó caída;
y cobrando nueva vida,
de tal manera he trocado
que mi Amado para mí,
y yo soy para mí Amado.

Tiróme con una flecha
enerbolada de amor,
y mi alma quedó hecha
una con su Criador.
Ya yo no quiero otro amor,
pues a mi Dios me he entregado,
y mi Amado para mí,
y yo soy para mí Amado.

My Beloved Is For Me

I gave myself so totally,
and the exchange has thus been done
that my Beloved is for me,
and I'm for only my Loved One.

When that sweet Hunter from above
had wounded and o'erpowered me,
and left me in the arms of love,
my soul abiding languidly;
new life came in recovery,
and the exchange has thus been done
that my Beloved is for me,
and I'm for only my Loved One.

The arrow used in wounding me
with his love he had deigned to fill,
and so my soul was made to be
at one with its Creator's will.
No other love could e'er fulfill,
since to my God surrender is done,
and my Beloved is for me,
and I'm for only my Loved One.

Vivo Sin Vivir En Mí

Vivo sin vivir en mí
y de tal manera espero,
que muero porque no muero.

Vivo ya fuera de mí,
después que muero de amor,
porque vivo en el Señor,
que me quiso para sí.
Cuando el corazón le di
puso en él este letrero:
que muero porque no muero.

Esta divina prisión,
del amor con que yo vivo,
ha hecho a Dios me cautivo.
Y libre mi corazón
y causa en mí tal pasión,
ver a Dios mi prisionero,
que muero porque no muero.

I Live Lacking Life In Me

I live lacking life in me,
and my hope is such I sigh,
that I die since I don't die.

I now live outside of me,
since I truly die of love,
living in the Lord above,
who wants me for him to be.
When I gave my heart, then he
deep within it wrote this cry:
that I die since I don't die.

So this prison heavenly,
of the love in which I live,
has made God my own captive.
And it makes my heart fly free
with such passion just to see
God, my prisoner, that is why
I now die since I don't die.

¡Ay, que larga es esta vida!
¡Que duros estos destierros!
Esta cárcel y estos hierros
en que el alma está metida!
Sólo esperar la salida
me causa un dolor tan fiero,
que muero porque no muero.

¡Ay, qué vida tan amarga
do no se goza el Señor!
Porque si es dulce el amor,
no lo es la esperanza larga.
Quíteme Dios esta carga,
más pesada que el acero,
que muero porque no muero.

Sólo con la confianza
vivo de que he de morir,
porque muriendo el vivir
me asegura mi esperanza.
Muerte do el vivir se alcanza,
no te tardes, que te espero,
que muero porque no muero.

Ah, how long this life I've found!
Hard this exile still remains!
In this jail and all these chains
by which this poor soul is bound!
Hoping just to leave this ground
brings such sorrow that I sigh,
that I die since I don't die.

Ah, this life is bitter fate
when the Lord I can't enjoy!
For love's sweetness starts to cloy,
when it suffers a long wait.
God my burden mitigate,
it's like heavy steel; I cry
that I die since I don't die.

Only since my faith assures
that I must die do I live,
for in dying hope does give
me belief that life endures.
Since it's life that death procures,
don't delay, I wait and sigh
that I die since I don't die.

Mira que el amor es fuerte.
Vida, no me seas molesta.
Mira que sólo me resta
para ganarte perderte.
Venga ya la dulce muerte,
el morir venga ligero.
Que muero porque no muero.

Aquella vida de arriba,
que es la vida verdadera,
hasta que esta vida muera,
no se goza estando viva.
Muerte, no me seas esquiva;
viva muriendo primero,
que muero porque no muero.

Vida, ¿que puedo yo darte
a mi Dios, que vive en mí,
si no es el perderte a ti,
para merecer ganarte?
Quiero muriendo alcanzarte,
pues tanto a mi amado quiero:
que muero porque no muero.

See how love has grown so strong.
Life, do not be troubling me.
See all that remains to be,
lose you now to gain you long.
Come sweet death, now hear my song,
swiftly come, my death, for I
know I die since I don't die.

Heavenly life for which we strive
is the truest life we know,
till death ends this mortal glow,
there's no joy to be alive.
Death come now, do not deprive;
in first dying, life draw nigh,
for I die since I don't die.

Life, what can I give to win
my dear God, who lives in me,
if not losing you it be,
for to merit gaining him?
Dying I would reach within
my beloved for whom I sigh
that I die since I don't die.

En Las Manos De Dios

Vuestra soy, para Vos nací,
¿Qué mandáis hacer de mí?

Soberana Majestad,
eterna sabiduría,
bondad buena al alma mía;
la gran vileza mirad
Dios, alteza, un ser, bondad.
Que hoy os canta amor así:
¿Qué mandáis hacer de mí?

Vuestra soy, pues me críastes,
Vuestra, pues me redimistes,
Vuestra, pues que me sufristes,
Vuestra, pues que me llamastes,
Vuestra, pues que me esperastes,
Vuestra, pues no me perdí.
¿Qué mandáis hacer de mí?

¿Que mandais, pues, buen Señor,
que haga tan vil criado?
¿Cual oficio le habéis dado
a este esclavo pecador?
Veisme aquí, mi dulce Amor,
Amor dulce, veisme aquí,
¿Qué mandáis hacer de mí?

In The Hands Of God

Yours I am, born yours to be,
what's your will to make of me?

Sovereign Majesty, decreeing
wisdom timeless, ever whole;
kindness pleasing to my soul;
God, most high, all good, one being,
this vile creature you are seeing,
who sings to you lovingly:
what's your will to make of me?

Yours, for me you did create,
Yours, since me you did succor,
Yours, since me you did endure,
Yours, you called me to my fate,
Yours, for me you did long wait,
Yours, I chose not lost to be.
What's your will to make of me?

What, then, is your will, good Lord,
that this servant vile should do?
What work can you give unto
this poor slave in sin abhorred?
Look at me, sweet Love adored,
sweet Love, here for you to see,
what's your will to make of me?

Veis aquí mi corazón,
yo le pongo en vuestra palma,
mi cuerpo, mi vida y alma,
mis entrañas y afición,
dulce Esposo y redención,
pues por vuestra me ofrecí,
¿Qué mandáis hacer de mí?

Dadme muerte, dadme vida,
dad salud o enfermedad,
honra o deshonra me dad,
dadme guerra o paz credida,
flaqueza o fuerza cumplida,
que a todo digo que sí,
¿Qué mandáis hacer de mí?

Dadme riqueza o pobreza,
dad consuelo o desconsuelo,
dadme alegría o tristeza,
dadme infierno o dadme cielo,
vida dulce, sol sin velo,
pues del todo me rendí.
¿Qué mandáis hacer de mí?

Si queréis, dadme oración,
si no, dadme sequedad,
si abundancia y devoción,
y si no esterilidad,
Soberana Majestad,
sólo hallo paz aquí.
¿Qué mandáis hacer de mí?

See my heart here for inspection,
I place it within your hand,
with my body, life, soul and
my deep feelings and affection,
sweetest Bridegroom and redemption,
myself offering yours to be,
what's your will to make of me?

Give me death, or let me live,
give health or infirmity,
shame or honor give to me,
war or peace to me now give,
weakness, strength superlative,
to all these I will agree,
what's your will to make of me?

Give me wealth or poverty,
give relief or troubled spell,
give me sorrow or give glee,
give me heaven or give me hell,
sweet life or sun without veil,
I surrender totally.
What's your will to make of me?

If you wish to, give me prayer,
if not, give me dryness too,
if abundant worship fair,
if not barrenness will do,
Sovereign Majesty, in you
I find all my peace to be.
What's your will to make of me?

Dadme, pues, sabiduría,
o por amor, ignorancia,
dadme años de abundancia,
o de hambre y carestía
dad tiniebla o claro día,
revolvedme aquí o allí.
¿Qué mandáis hacer de mí?

Si queréis que esté holgando,
quiero por amor holgar;
si me mandáis trabajar,
morir quiero trabajando.
Decid, ¿dónde, cómo y cuándo
decid, dulce Amor, decid.
¿Qué mandáis hacer de mí?

Dadme Calvario o Tabor,
desierto o tierra abundosa,
sea Job en el dolor,
o Juan que al pecho reposa;
sea viña fructuosa
o estéril, si cumple así.
¿Qué mandáis hacer de mí?

Sea José puesto en cadenas,
o de Egipto Adelantado
o David sufriendo penas,
o ya David encumbrado,
sea Jonás anegado,
o libertado de allí,
¿Qué mandáis hacer de mí?

Give me wisdom's deep insight,
or for love, just ignorance,
give me years of abundance,
or of hunger, famine's blight,
give me dark or clear daylight,
move me here or there freely.
What's your will to make of me?

If you wish that I should rest,
I, for love, want rest to savor;
if your will is that I labor,
death from work is my request.
Say where, how, when, manifest;
say, sweet Love, now say clearly.
What's your will to make of me?

Give me Tabor or Calvary,
desert or land fruitfully fine,
be as Job in misery,
or John, on your breast recline;
let me be a fruitful vine
or bare, as your will may be.
What's your will to make of me?

Be I Joseph placed in chains,
Egypt's governor of renown,
or as David suffering pains,
or now David bearing crown,
be I Jonah nearly drowned,
or from waters now set free,
what's your will to make of me?

Esté callando o hablando,
haga fruto o no le haga,
muéstrame la ley mi llaga,
goce de Evangelio blando;
esté penando o gozando,
sólo Vos en mi vivid,
¿Qué mandáis hacer de mí?

Vuestra soy, para Vos nací,
¿Qué mandáis hacer de mí?

Being silent, moved to speak,
bearing fruit or barren woe,
my wound to me law does show,
Gospel mild does joy bespeak;
mournful or enjoyment's peak,
in me now lives You only,
what's your will to make of me?

Yours I am, born yours to be,
what's your will to make of me?

El Camino De La Cruz

En la cruz está la vida
y el consuelo,
y ella sola es el camino
para el cielo.

En la cruz está el Señor
de cielo y tierra,
y el gozar de mucha paz,
aunque haya guerra.
Todos los males destierra
en este suelo,
y ella sola es el camino
para el cielo.

De la cruz dice la Esposa
a su Querido
que es una palma preciosa
donde ha subido
y su fruto le ha sabido
a Dios del cielo,
y ella sola es el camino
para el cielo.

The Way Of The Cross

Within the cross is life's mainstay
and consolation,
and it alone provides the way
to our salvation.

Upon the cross is hung the Lord
of heaven and of earth,
and it, despite the clash of sword,
to joy of peace gives birth;
of every evil making dearth
throughout creation;
and it alone provides the way
to our salvation.

From on the cross now would the bride
to her Beloved cry
how precious on this palm to bide
where she has climbed on high,
and whose dear fruit has brought her nigh
God's manifestation,
and it alone provides the way
to our salvation.

Es una oliva preciosa
la santa cruz,
que con su aceite no unta
y nos da luz.
Alma mía, toma la cruz
con gran consuelo,
y ella sola es el camino
para el cielo.

Es la cruz el árbol verde
y deseado
de la Esposa, que a su sombra
se ha sentado.
Para gozar de su Amado
El Rey del cielo,
y ella sola es el camino
para el cielo.

El alma que a Dios está
toda rendida,
y muy de veras del mundo
desasida,
la cruz le es árbol de vida
y de consuelo,
y ella sola es el camino
para el cielo.

Después que se puso en cruz
El Salvador,
en la cruz está la gloria
y el honor,
y en el padecer dolor
vida y consuelo,
y el camino más seguro
para el cielo.

This sacred cross becomes a precious
living olive tree,
that freely with its oil anoints us,
giving light to see.
My soul, take up this cross and be
with consolation,
for it alone provides the way
to our salvation.

This cross becomes the verdant tree
that's treasured by the bride;
securely in whose shadows she
can now in peace abide,
with joy, Beloved by her side,
King of creation;
and it alone provides the way
to our salvation.

The soul that unto God itself
has freely given,
and truly from the world and pelf
is fully riven,
finds tree of life from cross has thriven,
and consolation;
and it alone provides the way
to our salvation.

Our Savior having on the cross
his own self placed,
with glory, honor has this cross
by him been graced;
and in his suffering, life we taste,
and consolation,
and it provides the way most sure
to our salvation.

A La Cruz

Cruz, descanso sabroso de mi vida
vos seáis la bienvenida.

Oh, bandera, en cuyo amparo
el más flaco será fuerte;
oh, vida de nuestra muerte,
qué bien la has resucitado
al león has amansado.
Pues por ti perdió la vida,
vos seáis la bienvenida.

Quien no os ama está cautivo
y ajeno de libertad;
quien a vos quiere allegar
no tendrá en nada desvío.
Oh dichoso poderío,
donde el mal no halla cabida,
vos seáis la bienvenida.

Vos fuisteis la libertad
de nuestro gran cautiverio;
por vos se reparó mi mal
con tan costoso remedio
para con Dios fuiste medio
de alegría conseguida,
vos seáis la bienvenida.

To The Cross

Cross, my life's delight, tranquility,
let you my welcome be.

O standard, you so well protect
the feeblest, making hale;
O life from death prevail,
how well you resurrect,
the lion's fierceness checked.
By you he lost mortality,
let you my welcome be.

Who loves you not must e'er remain
a captive, never free;
who draws near you in unity
from evil you restrain.
Oh, happy is this blest domain,
for evil no capacity,
let you my welcome be.

You were the source of liberation
from our great captivity;
from our evil setting free
with such precious reparation,
through God was the mediation
for attaining ecstacy,
let you my welcome be.

Abrazadas A La Cruz

Caminemos para el cielo,
monjas del Carmelo.

Abracemos bien la Cruz
y sigamos a Jesús,
que es nuestro camino y luz
lleno de todo consuelo,
monjas del Carmelo.

Si guardáis más que los ojos
la profesión de tres votos,
libraros de mil enojos,
de tristeza y desconsuelo,
monjas del Carmelo.

El voto de la obediencia,
aunque es de muy alta ciencia,
jamás se la hace ofensa
sino cuando hay resistencia.
De ésta os libre Dios del cielo,
monjas del Carmelo.

Embracing the Cross

Unto heaven let us travel,
nuns of Carmel.

Let us now the cross embrace,
Jesus following apace,
he our way and light by grace,
giving consolation well,
nuns of Carmel.

One who guards more than the eyes,
with three vows professed complies,
frees the self from countless sighs
of distress and sorrow's spell,
nuns of Carmel.

First vow of obedience,
though of highest lore and sense,
only brings to one offense
when 'tis met with resistance.
Free us God from this as well,
nuns of Carmel.

El voto de castidad
con gran cuidado guardad.
A solo Dios desead,
y en El mismo os encerrad,
sin mirar cosa del suelo,
monjas del Carmelo.

El que llaman de pobreza,
si se guarda con pureza,
está lleno de riqueza
y abre las puertas del cielo,
monjas del Carmelo.

Y si así lo hacemos
los contrarios venceremos
y a la fin descansaremos
con el que hizo tierra y cielo,
monjas del Carmelo.

Second vow of chastity
guard with great security.
With God only seek to be,
earthly things disdain to see,
safely in God's citadel,
nuns of Carmel.

What they name as poverty,
if 'tis kept with purity,
filled with riches it will be,
opening heaven's gates to dwell,
nuns of Carmel.

And if we so pass the test
all opponents we will best,
and at last with him will rest
who made heaven and earth as well,
nuns of Carmel.

Hacia La Patria

Caminemos para el cielo,
monjas del Carmelo.

Vamos muy mortificadas,
humildes y despreciadas,
dejando el consuelo,
monjas del Carmelo.

Al voto de la obediencia
vamos, no haya resistencia,
que es nuestro blanco y consuelo,
monjas del Carmelo.

La pobreza es el camino,
el mismo por donde vino
nuestro Emperador del cielo,
monjas del Carmelo.

No deja de nos amar
nuestro Dios y nos llamar
sigámosle sin recelo,
monjas del Carmelo.

The Way To Heaven

Unto heaven let us travel,
nuns of Carmel.

Let us go in mortification,
humble and despised in station,
leave all consolation as well,
nuns of Carmel.

To our vowed obedience
let us go, with no resistence,
t'is our goal and soothing counsel,
nuns of Carmel.

Poverty the sure way, same
as the road by which he came,
heavenly Emperor, here to dwell,
nuns of Carmel.

Never ceasing in his love
God calls to us from above;
let us follow trusting well,
nuns of Carmel.

Un amor se está abrasando
aquel que nació temblando
envuelto en humano velo
monjas del Carmelo.

Vámonos a enriquecer,
a donde nunca ha de haber
pobreza ni desconsuelo,
monjas del Carmelo.

Al Padre Elías siguiendo
nos vamos contradiciendo
con su fortaleza y celo,
monjas del Carmelo.

Nuestro querer renunciando,
procuremos el doblado
espíritu de Eliseo,
monjas del Carmelo.

Love, whose fire was burning bright,
born a trembling babe one night,
veiled within the human shell,
nuns of Carmel.

Let us seek this wealth of grace,
never finding in that place
poverty nor grief should dwell,
nuns of Carmel.

Father Elijah following,
self-denial like his we bring,
strength and zeal that none can quell,
nuns of Carmel.

All desires renounced, we long
for the double spirit strong
that upon Elisha fell,
nuns of Carmel.

Al Nacimiento De Jesús

¡Ah, pastores que veláis,
por guardar vuestros rebaños,
mirad que os nace un Cordero,
Hijo de Dios Soberano!

Viene pobre y despreciado,
comenzadle ya a guardar,
que a lobo os le ha de llevar
sin que le hayamos gozado.
— Gil, dame acá aquel cayado
que no me saldrá de mano,
no nos lleven al Cordero:
— *¿No ves que es Dios Soberano?*

¡Sonzas! Que estoy aturdido
de gozo y de penas junto.
— ¿Si es Dios el que hoy ha nacido,
cómo puede ser difunto?
¡Oh, que es hombre también junto!
La vida estará en su mano;
mirad, que es este el Cordero,
Hijo de Dios Soberano.

To the Birth of Jesus

Ah, you shepherds keeping watch,
guard your flocks, all dangers ward,
look for you is born a Lamb,
Son of God our Sovereign Lord!

Coming poor, despised is he,
guard him now with watchful care,
lest a wolf take him from there,
ere we know him joyfully.
  — Gil, your crook, now give to me,
firmly held, it will afford
to protect from theft the Lamb:
  — *see not he's our Sovereign Lord?*

Zounds! I am bewildered now,
joy and sorrow joined in me.
  — If 'tis God born here, then how
can he know mortality?
Oh, his too, humanity!
Life is his to yield or hoard;
look, this truly is the Lamb,
Son of God our Sovereign Lord!

No sé para qué le piden,
pues le dan después tal guerra;
— mía fe, Gil, mejor será
que se nos torne a su tierra,
si el pecado nos destierra,
y está el bien todo en su mano.
Ya que ha venido padezca
este Dios tan soberano.

Poco te duele su pena;
¡Oh, como es cierto, del hombre
cuando nos viene provecho,
el mal ajeno se esconde!
¿No ves que gana renombre
de pastor de gran rebaño?
Con todo, es cosa muy fuerte
que muera Dios Soberano.

Why for him their every plea,
since against him war they start;
— Gil, in truth, 'twould better be
for him from us to depart,
if our sin keeps us apart.
In his hand all good reward,
since he came for us to suffer
this God is our Sovereign Lord.

Little you regret his pain;
oh, how true, men have profaned,
when to us comes worldly gain,
others' suffering is disdained!
See not what renown he gained,
shepherd of his flock adored?
Terrible 'tis nonethess
that he dies, our Sovereign Lord.

Al Nacimiento De Jesús

Hoy nos viene a redimir
un Zagal, nuestra pariente,
Gil, que es Dios omnipotente.

Por eso nos ha sacado
de prisión a Satanás;
mas es pariente de Bras,
y de Menga, y de Llorente.
¡Oh, que es Dios omnipotente!

Pues si es Dios, ¿como es vendido
y muere crucificado?
— ¿No ves que mató el pecado,
padeciendo el inocente?
Gil, que es Dios omnipotente.

Mi fe, yo lo vi nacido
de una muy linda Zagala.
— Pues si es Dios ¿como ha querido
estar con tan pobre gente?
— *¿No ves, que es omnipotente?*

Déjate de esas preguntas,
muramos por le servir,
y pues El viene a morir
muramos con El, Llorente,
pues es Dios omnipotente.

At the Birth of Jesus

Our redeemer comes today, a
shepherd boy, our kin is sent,
Gil, he's God omnipotent.

Therefore he has set us free from
Satan's prison of our sin;
but of Bras he is the kin,
and of Menga, and Llorente.
Oh, he's God omnipotent.

If he's God, how is he sold,
crucified and made to die?
— See you not, sin was killed by
suffering of this innocent?
Gil, he's God omnipotent.

True, his birth was seen by me,
of a lovely shepherdess.
— If he's God, why choose to be
born by folk of poor descent?
See not he's omnipotent?

Cease from all your questioning,
now to serve him let us fly,
and since he has come to die
let us die with him, Llorente,
since he's God omnipotent.

Para Navidad

Pues el amor
nos ha dado Dios,
ya no hay que temer,
muramos los dos.

Danos el Padre
a su único Hijo;
hoy viene al mundo
en un pobre cortijo.
¡Oh, gran regocijo,
que ya el hombre es Dios!
No hay que temer,
muramos los dos.

Mira, Llorente
qué fuerte amorío,
viene el inocente
a padecer frío;
deja un señorío
en fin, como Dios,
No hay que temer,
muramos los dos.

For Christmas

Since love gave us God,
now both you and I
have no need to fear,
so let us both die.

The Father is giving
us his only Son;
to all the world's living,
in stable 'twas done.
Oh, joy now begun,
that man deify!
There's no need to fear,
so let us both die.

Observe now, Llorente,
with love that is bold
comes the innocent
to suffer the cold;
yields lordship untold
as God from on high,
there's no need to fear,
so let us both die.

Pues, ¿como, Pascual,
hizo esa franqueza,
que toma un sayal
dejando riqueza?
Mas quiere pobreza,
Sigámosle nos;
pues ya viene hombre,
muramos los dos.

Pues, ¿que le daran
por esta grandeza?
Grandes azotes
con mucha crudeza.
Oh, qué gran tristeza
será para nos:
si esto es verdad,
muramos los dos.

Pues ¿cómo se atreven
siendo Omnipotente?
Ha de ser muerto
de una mala gente.
Pues si eso es, Llorente;
hurtémosle nos,
no ves que El lo quiere,
muramos los dos.

Pascual, why this course
he took graciously,
to wear clothes so coarse
and none lavishly?
He sought poverty,
let's follow him nigh;
Since he became man,
then let us both die.

Then what should we give
for one that's so great?
The lash punitive
with cruelty and hate.
Oh, sorrowful fate
to be you and I;
if this should be true
then let us both die.

How do they not dread
the Omnipotent?
Those making him dead
are malevolent.
If true then, Llorente,
steal him we must try,
see not that he wills it,
then let us both die.

Al Nacimiento Del Niño Dios

Mi gallejo, mira quién llama.
Angeles son, que ya viene el alba.

Hame dad un gran zumbido
que parece cantillana,
mira Bras, que ya es de día,
vamos a ver la zagala.
Mi gallejo, mira quién llama.
Angeles son, que ya viene el alba.

¿Es parienta del alcalde,
u quién es esta doncella?
Ella es hija de Dios Padre,
Relumbra, como una estrella.
Mi gallejo, mira quién llama.
Angeles son, que ya viene el alba.

At the Birth of the Infant God

My Gallejo, look who's calling,
Angels all, now comes the dawn.

Greatly ringing in my ear, a
song is what it seems to be,
look, Bras, for the day is here, the
shepherdess let's go to see.
My Gallejo, look who's calling,
Angels all, now comes the dawn.

Is she relative of Mayor,
just who could this maiden be?
Like a star in sparkling splendor,
God the Father's daughter she.
My Gallejo, look who's calling,
Angels all, now comes the dawn.

A La Circuncisión

Vertiendo está sangre,
¡Dominguillo, eh!
Yo no sé por qué.

¿Por qué, te pregunto,
hacen dél justicia,
pues es inocente
y no tiene malicia?
Tuvo gran codicia,
yo no sé por qué,
de mucho amarme,
¡Dominguillo, eh!

¿Pues luego en naciendo,
le han de atormentar?
— Sí, que está muriendo
por quitar el mal;
¡Oh, que gran Zagal
será, por mi fe!
¡Dominguillo, eh!

¿Tú no lo has mirando,
que es niño inocente?
— Ya me lo han contado
Brasillo y Llorente;
gran inconveniente
será no amalle,
¡Dominguillo, eh!

On The Circumcision

He is shedding blood,
Dominguillo, oh!
Why I do not know.

Why, I ask of you,
do they judge when he
is so pure and true,
no malignity?
Great his thirst for me,
why I do not know,
he should love me so,
Dominguillo, oh!

After his birth, why
must they castigate?
— Yes, for he would die,
sin to abrogate.
Oh, he'll be a great
Shepherd, this I know!
Dominguillo, oh!

This child, did you see,
that he's innocent?
— They have told to me,
Brasillo and Llorente;
what great detriment
if you love him no,
Dominguillo, oh!

Otra A La Circuncisión

Este Niño viene llorando;
mírale, Gil, que te está llamando.

Vino del cielo a la tierra
para quitar nuestra guerra;
ya comienza la pelea,
su sangre está derramando,
mírale, Gil, que te está llamando.

Fue tan grande, el amorío,
que no es mucho estar llorando,
que comienza a tener brío,
habiendo de estar mandando.
Mírale, Gil, que te está llamando.

Caro nos ha de costar,
pues comienza tan temprano,
a su sangre derramar,
habremos de estar llorando
mírale, Gil, que te está llamando.

No viniera El a morir
pues podría estarse en su nido,
¿no ves, Gil, que si ha venido
es como león bramando?
Mírale, Gil, que te está llamando.

Another On The Circumcision

This child, crying, comes in view;
look, Gil, he is calling you.

Down to earth from heaven he came,
all our warring ways to tame,
now the battle starts to flame,
his blood he is shedding too,
look, Gil, he is calling you.

Greatly he did love bestow,
'tis no wonder tears should flow,
now his strength begins to grow,
he must be commander too.
Look, Gil, he is calling you.

Dear for us the price will be,
since beginning so early,
shedding blood for you and me,
from us also tears are due,
look, Gil, he is calling you.

Think you not he comes to die,
not stay home, be safe thereby;
Gil, he comes, don't you descry,
like a lion roaring through?
Look, Gil, he is calling you.

Dime Pascual, ¿que me quieres,
que tantos gritos me das?
Que le ames, pues te quiere,
y por ti está tiritando;
mírale, Gil, que te está llamando.

Pascual, what you want, tell me,
why such shouting noisily?
Love him as he loves you, see
that for you he shivers too;
look, Gil, he is calling you.

Ayes Del Destierro

¡Cuan triste es, Dios mío,
la vida sin ti!
Ansiosa de verte,
deseo morir.

Carrera muy larga
es la de este suelo,
morada penosa,
muy duro destierro.
¡Oh Dueñoadorado!
Sácame de aquí.
Ansiosa de verte,
deseo morir.

Lúgubre es la vida,
amarga en extremo;
que no vive el alma
que está de ti lejos.
¡Oh dulce bien mío,
que soy infeliz!
Ansiosa de verte,
deseo morir.

Sighs in Exile

How dismal, my God, is
this life without you!
So eager to see you,
I long for to die.

A course very long is
the life on this earth; it's
a dwelling most painful,
an exile oppressive.
Oh Lord, my adored one,
remove me from here!
So eager to see you,
I long for to die.

Life truly is mournful,
most bitter as can be;
the soul is not living
that from you is distant.
Oh my sweetest goodness,
how sad that I am!
So eager to see you,
I long for to die.

¡Oh muerte benigna
socorre mis penas!
Tus golpes son dulces,
que el alma libertan.
¡Que dicha, oh mi amado,
estar junto a Ti!
Ansiosa de verte,
deseo morir.

El amore mundano
apega a esta vida;
el amor divino
por la otra suspira.
Sin ti, Dios eterno,
¿quien puede vivir?
Ansiosa de verte,
deseo morir.

La vida terrena
es continuo duelo;
vida verdadera
la hay sólo en el cielo.
Permite, Dios mío,
que viva yo allí,
ansiosa de verte,
deseo morir.

¿Quien es el que teme
la muerte del cuerpo,
si con ella logra
un placer inmenso?
¡Oh! sí, el de amarte,
Dios mío, sin fin.
Ansiosa de verte,
deseo morir.

Oh merciful death won't
you aid my affliction!
Your blows striking gently,
my soul they are freeing.
What joy, my beloved,
to be joined with you!
So eager to see you,
I long for to die.

The love that is worldly
to this life adheres; but
the love that's divine
for the other life sighs.
God eternal, who can live,
without you be nigh?
So eager to see you,
I long for to die.

The life of this world is
a ne'er ending sorrow;
the life lived in truth is
found only in heaven.
Allow it, my God, that
my life may be there,
so eager to see you,
I long for to die.

Who is it that's fearing
the death of the body,
if by that is gaining
a pleasure unbounded?
Oh, yes, just to love you,
my God, without end!
So eager to see you,
I long for to die.

Mi alma afligida
gime y desfallece.
¡Ay! ¿Quien de su amado
puede estar ausente?
Acabe ya, acabe
aqueste sufrir,
ansiosa de verte,
deseo morir.

El barbo cogido
en doloso anzuelo,
encuentra en la muerte
el fin del tormento.
¡Ay! Tambien yo sufro,
bien mío, sin ti:
ansiosa de verte,
deseo morir.

En vano mi alma
te busca, oh mi dueño;
tu siempre invisible
no alivias su anhelo.
¡Ay! Esto la inflama
hasta prorrumpir:
ansiosa de verte,
deseo morir.

My soul is afflicted
with groaning and fainting.
Ah, who from their loved one
can bear to be absent?
Now bring to completion
this suffering, for I
am eager to see you,
and long for to die.

The fish that is caught by
the fishhook's deception,
will find in its death all
the end to its torment.
Ah, how I too suffer,
my good, without you:
so eager to see you,
I long for to die.

In vain does my soul for
you seek, oh my master;
to find you unseen, no
relief from my longing.
Ah, this so inflames me
until I must cry:
so eager to see you,
I long for to die.

¡Ay! Cuando te dignas
entrar en mi pecho,
Dios mío, al instante
el perderte temo.
Tal pena me aflige,
y me hace decir:
ansiosa de verte,
deseo morir.

Haz, Señor, que acabe
tan larga agonía;
socorre a tu sierva
que por ti suspira.
Rompe aquestos hierros
y sea feliz.
Ansiosa de verte,
deseo morir.

Mas no, dueño amado,
que es justo padezca;
que expíe mis yerros,
mis culpas inmensas.
¡Ay! Logren mis lágrimas
te dignes oír:
ansiosa de verte,
deseo morir.

Ah, when you vouchsafe to
come into my heart, at
that instant, my God, I
feel fear of your leaving.
Such pain that afflicts me,
and makes me now sigh:
so eager to see you,
I long for to die.

Lord, now make an end to
this anguish of mine and
give aid to your servant
who sighs for you only.
Break through all these shackles,
let happiness be.
So eager to see you,
I long for to die.

But no, beloved master,
it's just that I suffer;
my sins to atone for,
my guilt so enormous.
Ah, may my tears gain that
you deign hear my sigh:
so eager to see you,
I long for to die.

En La Festividad De Los Santos Reyes

Pues la estrella
es ya llegada,
vaya con los Reyes
la mi manada.

Vamos todos juntos
a ver el Mesías,
pues vemos cumplidas
ya las profecías;
pues en nuestros días,
es ya llegada,
vaya con los Reyes
la mi manada.

Llevémosle dones
de grande valor,
pues vienen los Reyes
con tan gran hervor.
Alégrese hoy
nuestra gran Zagala,
vaya con los Reyes
la mi manada.

On The Feast Of The Holy Kings

The star has arrived,
to guide with its glow;
along with the Kings,
my flock, you must go.

Let's all go together
Messiah to see,
we will see fulfillment
of each prophecy;
in our day comes he,
foretold long ago,
along with the Kings,
my flock, you must go.

Let's bring to him gifts of
a value most great;
the Kings, full of ardor,
are coming in state.
May all this elate
our shepherdess, so
along with the Kings,
my flock, you must go.

No cures, Llorente,
de buscar razón,
para ver que es Dios
aqueste garzón;
dale el corazon,
y yo esté empeñada,
vaya con los Reyes
la mi manada.

Don't bother, Llorente, to
search rationally
in order for God in
this young boy to see.
Give him your heart free;
and I, all will owe,
along with the Kings,
my flock, you must go.

A San Andrés

¿Si el padecer con amor
puede dar tan gran deleite?
¡Que gozo nos dara el verte!

¿Qué será cuando veamos
a la eterna Majestad,
pues de ver Andrés la cruz
se pudo tanto alegrar?
¡Oh, que no puede faltar
en el padecer deleite!
¡Que gozo nos dara el verte!

El amor cuando es crecido
no puede estar sin obrar,
ni el fuerte sin pelear,
por amor de su Querido.
Con esto le habrá vencido,
y querrá que en todo acierte,
¡Que gozo nos dara el verte!

To Saint Andrew

If suffering for the sake of love
can give delight so wondrously,
What joy 'twill give us you to see!

What will it be when we're beholding
everlasting Majesty,
since Andrew when he came to see
the cross found joy within unfolding.
Oh, that there be no withholding
of delight in misery!
What joy 'twill give us you to see!

A love, when it is fully grown,
unless it works cannot exist,
a fighter so must use his fist,
for his Beloved's love to own.
By this the victory is known,
and always wanting right to be,
what joy 'twill give us you to see!

Pues todos temen la muerte
¿como te es dulce el morir?
¡O, que voy para vivir
en más encumbrada suerte!
¡Oh mi Dios! Que con tu muerte
al más flaco hiciste fuerte:
¡Que gozo nos dara el verte!

¡Oh Cruz! Madero, precioso
lleno de gran majestad,
pues siendo de despreciar
tomaste a Dios por esposo.
A ti vengo muy gozoso,
sin merecer el quererte.
¡Que gozo nos dara el verte!

Since every person fears to die
why does your dying sweetness give?
Oh, I will ever seek to live
in ways that elevate more high!
For, oh my God, because you die,
the weakest is made strong to be:
what joy 'twill give us you to see!

Oh Cross, your precious wood o'ercome
with greatest majesty, you rise
where once your sight all would despise,
for God your spouse has now become.
To you most joyfully I come,
though loving you unworthily.
What joy 'twill give us you to see!

A San Hilarion

Hoy vencido un guerrero
al mundo y a sus valedores.
Vuelta, vuelta, pecadores,
sigamos este sendero.

Sigamos la soledad
y no queramos morir,
hasta ganar el vivir
en tan subida pobreza.
¡Oh, qué grande es la destreza
de aquéste nuestro guerrero!
Vuelta, vuelta, pecadores,
sigamos este sendero.

Con armas de penitencia
ha vencido a Lucifer,
combate con la paciencia,
ya no tiene que temer.
Todos podemos valer
siguiendo este caballero,
vuelta, vuelta, pecadores,
sigamos este sendero.

To Saint Hilarion

Warrior conquers on this day,
all the world and its defenders.
Turn, turn back from sin, offenders,
let us follow in this way.

Seeking solitude let's be,
ceasing all desire to die,
till we gain the true life by
gaining deepest poverty.
Oh, great the dexterity
that our warrior can display!
Turn, turn back from sin, offenders,
let us follow in this way.

Being only armed with penance
he has conquered Lucifer,
fighting on with greatest patience,
having not a thing to fear.
We'll defend all we hold dear,
following this knight today,
turn, turn back from sin, offenders,
let us follow in this way.

No ha tenido valedores,
abrazóse con la cruz:
siempre en ella hallamos luz
pues la dio a los pecadores.
¡Oh, qué dichosos amores
tuvo este nuestro guerrero!
Vuelta, vuelta, pecadores,
sigamos este sendero.

Ya ha ganado la corona,
y se acabó el padecer,
gozando ya el merecer,
con muy encumbrada gloria.
¡Oh venturosa victoria
de nuestro fuerte guerrero!
Vuelta, vuelta, pecadores,
sigamos este sendero.

He, alone, without defenders,
cross embraced to set all right;
always in it we find light,
for us sinners that he renders.
Oh, what happy love, the splendors
that our warrior would display!
Turn, turn back from sin, offenders,
let us follow in this way.

Now he bears the crown he won,
and his suffering is past,
meriting this joy at last;
with high glory it was done.
Fortunate the victory won
by our warrior strong this day!
Turn, turn back from sin, offenders,
let us follow in this way.

A Santa Catalina Martir

¡Oh gran amadora
del Eterno Dios
estrella luciente,
amparadnos vos!

Desde tierna edad
tomaste Esposo
fue tanto el amor,
que no os dio reposo.
Quien es temeroso,
no se llegue a Vos,
si estima la vida
y el morir por Vos.

Mirad los cobardes
aquesta doncella,
que no estima el oro
ni verse tan bella.
Metida en la guerra
de persecución,
para padecer
con gran corazón.

To Saint Catherine, Martyr

Oh star shining brightly
with greatest affection
for God the eternal,
give us your protection!

At tenderest age you
took Spouse to your breast;
so strong was your love that
it gave you no rest.
Whom fear has distressed
won't come unto You,
if valuing life more
than dying through You.

You cowards behold
this little young maid,
who values not gold,
nor beauty displayed;
in war not afraid,
persecution her fate,
she suffers it all
with heart truly great.

Mas pena le da
vivir sin su Esposo
y así en los tormentos
hallaba reposo:
todo le es gozoso,
querría ya morir,
pues que con la vida
no puede vivir.

Las que pretendemos
gozar de su gozo,
nunca nos cansemos,
por hallar reposo,
¡Oh engaño engañoso,
y que sin amor,
es querer sanar,
viviendo el dolor!

More pain it would give,
her spouse to divest,
and so in great torment
she now finds her rest;
with joy she is blest,
now longing to die,
no more in this life
can I live, she would sigh.

And we now aspiring
her joy to possess
can't find ourselves tiring
in seeking our rest.
Oh fraud manifest,
that love to disdain,
desiring the healing
while living the pain!

A La Vestición De La Hermana
Jerónima De La Encarnación

¿Quién os trajo acá doncella,
del valle de la tristura?
— Dios y mi buena ventura.

For the Clothing of Sister Jerónima De La Encarnación

Who has brought you here young lady,
from the vale of sad misfortune?
— It is God and my good fortune.

Al Velo de la Hermana Isabel de los Angeles

Hermana, porque veléis,
os han dado hoy este velo,
y no os va menos que el cielo;
por eso, no os descuidéis.

Aqueste velo gracioso
os dice que estéis en vela,
guardando la centinela
hasta que venga el Esposo,
que, como ladron famoso,
vendrá cuando no penséis;
por eso, no os descuidéis.

No sabe nadie a cuál hora,
si en la vigilia primera
o en la segunda o tercera,
todo cristiano lo ignora.
Pues velad, velad, hermana,
no os roben lo que tenéis;
por eso, no os descuidéis.

For the Veiling of Sister Isabel de los Angeles

Sister, that you watchful be,
you are given now this veil,
that your walk to heaven prevail;
for that, act not carelessly.

By this graceful veil you claim
that a vigil you will keep,
watchful sentry spurning sleep,
lest you find the Bridegroom came,
secretly like thief of fame,
coming unexpectedly;
for that, act not carelessly.

Hour of coming none can know,
in what watch of night 'twill be,
first, or second, or tertiary;
every Christian can't foreknow.
Sister, watch, watch high and low,
lose not all to robbery;
for that, act not carelessly.

En vuestra mano encendida
tened siempre una candela,
y estad con el velo en vela,
las renes muy bien ceñidas.
No estéis siempre amodorrida,
catad que peligraréis.
por eso, no os descuidéis.

Tened olio en la aceitera
de obras y merecer,
para poder proveer
la lámpara, que no se muera;
porque quedaréis de fuera
si entonces no lo tenéis;
por eso, no os descuidéis.

Nadie os le dará prestado;
y si lo vais a comprar,
podríaseos tardar,
y el Esposo haber entrado,
y desque una vez cerrado,
no hay entrar aunque llaméis;
por eso, no os descuidéis.

Tened continuo cuidado
de cumplir con alma fuerte,
hasta el día de la muerte,
lo que habéis hoy profesado;
porque habiendo así velado
con el Esposo entraréis.
por eso, no os descuidéis.

In your hand a candle keep,
always have it burning bright;
veiled, in vigil, through the night,
and well girded in the deep
darkness ever fighting sleep,
danger a reality,
for that, act not carelessly.

Have your oil jar always nigh,
deeds and merit full inside,
to be able to provide
flame for lamp that will not die;
lest his coming pass you by
if you have no lamp to see;
for that, act not carelessly.

Nobody will lend you more;
and if you should go to buy,
but delay, you may descry
that the Spouse has come before,
then, when they have closed the door,
you're outside despite your plea;
for that, act not carelessly.

Have care always to obey,
to fulfill with strength of soul,
till the day death takes its toll,
what you have professed this day;
for in keeping watch this way,
with the Bridegroom you will be;
for that, act not carelessly.

A La Profesión De Isabel de los Angeles

Sea mi gozo en el llanto,
sobresalto mi reposo,
mi sosiego doloroso,
y mi bonanza el quebranto.

Entre borrascas mi amor,
y mi regalo en la herida,
esté en la muerte mi vida,
y en desprecios mi favor.

Mis tesoros en pobreza,
y mi triunfo en pelear,
mi descanso en trabajar,
y mi contento en tristeza.

En la oscuridad mi luz,
mi grandeza en puesto bajo.
De mi camino el atajo
y mi gloria sea la cruz.

Mi honra sea el abatimiento,
y mi palma padecer,
en las menguas mi crecer,
y en menoscabo mi aumento.

For the Profession of Isabel de los Angeles

Be my joy in tears' distress,
sudden dread my deep repose,
calmness in affliction's throes,
my success in brokenness.

Midst the storms may my love grow,
and my gift in injury,
within death let my life be,
in contempt my favors know.

My wealth be in poverty,
and my triumph in contending,
my rest in the work unending,
pleasure in melancholy.

My light in obscurity,
greatness in the place that's low.
By short cut the way I go,
and the cross my glory be.

Honor in humility,
and in suffering, palm of mine,
and my growth from my decline,
every loss a gain to me.

En el hambre mi hartura,
mi esperanza en el temor,
mis regalos en pavor,
mis gustos en amargura.

En olvido mi memoria,
mi alteza en humillación,
en bajeza mi opinión,
en afrenta mi vitoria.

Mi lauro esté en el desprecio,
en las penas mi afición,
mi dignidad sea el rincón,
y la soledad mi aprecio.

En Cristo mi confianza
y de El sólo mi asimiento,
en sus consancios mi aliento
y en su imitación mi holganza.

Aquí estriba mi firmeza,
aquí mi seguridad,
la prueba de mi verdad,
la muestra de mi fineza.

Hope be mine in what gives fright,
hunger be fulfilling bread,
all my gifts in what I dread,
bitterness be my delight.

In forgetting, memory,
highness in humiliation,
lowliness my reputation,
in affronts my victory.

Glory mine in others' scorn,
hardship be my inclination,
dignity in lowly station,
in aloneness honor born.

In Christ my reliance be,
attached to no thing but his figure,
in his weariness my vigor,
in his path tranquility.

Here my base of potency,
here is my security,
proof of my integrity,
guide to all my purity.

A Una Profesa

¡Oh! dichosa tal zagala
que hoy se ha dado a un tal Zagal
que reina y ha de reinar.

Venturosa fue su suerte
pues mereció tal Esposo.
Ya yo, Gil, estoy medroso,
no la osaré más mirar,
pues ha tomado marido
que reina y ha de reinar.

Pregúntale qué le ha dado
para que lleve a su aldea
el corazón le ha entregado
muy de buena voluntad.
Mi fe, poco le ha pagado
que es muy hermoso el Zagal,
que reina y ha de reinar.

Si más tuviera más diera.
¿Por qué le avisas, carillo?
Tomemos el cobanillo,
sirva nos deja sacar,
pues ha tomado marido,
que reina y ha de reinar.

To A Professed Nun

Oh, the happy shepherdess,
given this day to such a Shepherd
who now reigns and is to reign.

Such good fortune hers to gain,
that this Spouse she should deserve.
Gil, I fear now to observe
and her vision entertain,
since she took herself a husband
who now reigns and is to reign.

Ask her what gift she would fain
give him to take to his farm,
just her heart, she would explain,
offered with good will to charm.
What small price paid to attain
to that Shepherd very handsome,
who now reigns and is to reign.

If she gives all that remain,
why admonish her at all?
Let us take this basket small,
that she brings us to retain,
since a husband she has taken
who now reigns and is to reign.

Pues vemos lo que dio ella,
¿que le ha de dar el Zagal?
Con su sangre le ha comprado;
¡Oh que precioso caudal,
y dichosa tal zagala
que reina y ha de reinar.

Mucho le debía amar,
pues le dio tan gran tesoro,
¿no ves que se lo da todo
hasta el vestir y calzar?
Mira que es ya su marido
que reina y ha de reinar.

Bien será que la tomemos,
para este nuestro rebaño,
y que la regocijemos
para ganar su amistad,
pues ha tomado marido,
que reina y ha de reinar.

Since we see her gift, explain
what the Shepherd gave to her.
With his blood he purchased her.
Oh, what precious wealth to gain,
happy shepherdess to be with
who now reigns and is to reign.

She owes much love for his pain,
since he gave her such a treasure.
See you not he gave full measure,
left her clothed and shod again?
See that he is now her husband
who now reigns and is to reign.

Well it be that we ordain
her within our flock to be,
doing it delightedly,
that her friendship we may gain,
since a husband she has taken
who now reigns and is to reign.

En Una Profesión

¡Oh que bien tan sin segundo!
¡Oh casamiento sagrado!
Que el Rey de la Majestad,
haya sido el desposado.

¡Oh que venturosa suerte,
os estaba aparejada,
que os quiere Dios por amada,
y haos ganado con su muerte!
En servirle estad muy fuerte,
pues que los habéis profesado,
que el Rey de la Majestad,
es ya vuestro desposado

Ricas joyas os dará
este Esposo, Rey del cielo
daros ha mucho consuelo,
que nadie os lo quitará,
y sobre todo os dará
un espíritu humillado.
Es Rey y bien lo podrá,
pues quiere hoy ser desposado.

In A Profession

Oh what good, without an equal!
Oh what marital sanctity!
That the King of Majesty,
has become a spouse to be.

Oh what fortune sanctifying,
readied for you from above,
that God wants you for his love,
and has won you by his dying!
Serve him with all strength applying,
for the vows you took decree,
that the King of Majesty,
now becomes your spouse to be.

Richest jewels he'll give to you,
this your Spouse, the heavenly King,
giving you much comforting,
no one can this gift undo,
and o'er all he'll give you too
spirit of humility.
By the King's authority
he wants now a spouse to be.

Mas os dará este Señor,
un amor tan santo y puro,
que podréis, yo os lo asiguro,
perder al mundo el temor,
y al demonio muy mejor
porque hoy queda maniatado;
que el Rey de la Majestad,
ha sido hoy el desposado.

More, the Lord will give his dear,
love so holy and so pure,
that you can, I most assure,
lose all trace of worldly fear,
and, much more, the devil drear
handcuffed for eternity;
that the King of Majesty,
is today a spouse to be.

Para Una Profesión

Todos los que militáis
debajo desta bandera,
ya no durmáis, ya no durmáis,
pues ya no hay paz en la tierra.

Si como capitán fuerte
quiso nuestro Dios morir,
comencémosle a seguir
pues que le dimos la muerte,
oh qué venturosa suerte
se le siguió desta guerra;
ya no durmáis, ya no durmáis,
pues Dios falta de la tierra.

Con grande contentamiento
se ofrece a morir en cruz,
por darnos a todos luz
con su grande sufrimiento.
¡Oh, glorioso vencimiento!
¡Oh, dichosa aquesta guerra!
Ya no durmáis, ya no durmáis,
pues Dios falta de la tierra.

For A Profession

All in arms, profession keeping
'neath this banner fearlessly,
now no sleeping, now no sleeping,
peace on earth has ceased to be.

If as captain from on high
our God wishes to be dead,
let us follow where he led,
since we caused that he should die;
oh what luck we can descry
from this war that comes to be;
now no sleeping, now no sleeping,
God on earth has ceased to be.

With contentment truly great
on the cross he comes to die,
gives us all his light thereby,
with great suffering his fate.
Glorious win to celebrate!
Oh, this war ends happily!
Now no sleeping, now no sleeping,
God on earth has ceased to be.

No haya ningún cobarde,
aventuremos la vida,
pues no hay quien mejor la guarde
que el que la da por perdida.
Pues Jesús es nuestra guía,
y el premio de aquesta guerra;
ya no durmáis, ya no durmáis,
porque no hay paz en la tierra.

Ofrezcámonos de veras
a morir por Cristo todas,
y en las celestiales bodas,
estaremos placenteras;
sigamos estas banderas
pues Cristo va en delantera,
no hay que temer, no durmáis,
pues que no hay paz en la tierra.

Let no coward interfere,
let us bravely risk our life,
one best guards it from the strife
who will lose it with no fear.
Since our guide is Jesus here,
and this war's reward is he;
now no sleeping, now no sleeping,
peace on earth has ceased to be.

Let's present ourselves truly,
all of us for Christ to die,
and in heavenly wedding tie
ourselves to him joyfully;
following these banners free,
for Christ leads us faithfully,
fear no thing, and be not sleeping,
peace on earth has ceased to be.

En Una Profesión (2)

Pues que nuestro Esposo
nos quiere en prisión,
a la gala gala
de la Religión.

Oh qué ricas bodas
ordenó Jesús;
quiérenos a todas,
y danos la luz;
sigamos la cruz,
con gran perfección;
a la gala gala
de la Religión.

Este es el estado
de Dios escogido
con que del pecado
nos ha defendido;
hanos prometido
la consolación,
si nos alegramos
en esta prisión.
A la gala gala
de la Religión.

In A Profession (2)

Since it is our Spouse
wishing us in prison,
let us glory, glory
within our religion.

Oh what nuptial splendors
Jesus has ordained;
love to all he renders,
gives light unrestrained;
following cross we gained,
with such great perfection;
let us glory, glory
within our religion.

This to be the state
which for us God chose,
from our sinful fate
his defenses rose;
promising to those
consolation's vision
who are found rejoicing
being in this prison.
Let us glory, glory
within our religion.

Darnos ha grandezas
en la eterna gloria
si por sus riquezas
dejamos la escoria,
que hay en este mundo,
y su perdición,
a la gala gala
de la Religión.

Oh qué cautiverio
de gran libertad,
venturosa vida
para eternidad;
no quiero librar
ya mi corazón.
A la gala gala
de la Religión.

Grandeur he will give,
glory through the cross,
if for this we live
giving up the dross,
worldly things a loss,
and all their perdition,
let us glory, glory
within our religion.

Oh captivity
of freedom so great,
lucky life to be
this eternal fate;
not to liberate
my heart from its vision.
Let us glory, glory
within our religion.

Contra Un Ganadillo Impertinente

Pues nos dais vestido nuevo
Rey celestial,
librad de la mala gente
este sayal.

La Santa:
Hijas, pues tomáis la cruz,
tened valor,
y a Jesús, que es vuestra luz,
pedid favor.
El os será defensor
en trance tal.

Todos:
Librad de la mala gente
este sayal.

La Santa:
Inquieta este mal ganado
en oración,
el ánimo mal fundado,
en devoción;
mas en Dios el corazón
tened igual.

Against An Impertinent Little Flock

Since you give to us new clothing,
our heavenly King,
free this cloth of wool now from
each evil thing.

The Saint:
Daughters, since the cross you take,
have bravery,
Jesus will your light now make,
ask him your plea.
Your defender he will be
when dangers spring.

All:
Free this cloth of wool now from
each evil thing.

The Saint:
These bad creatures have confounded
one's prayer if she
has a spirit poorly founded
in piety;
yet in God hearts come to be
all equaling.

Todos:
Librad de la mala gente
este sayal.

La Santa:
Pues vinisteis a morir
no desmayéis,
y de gente tan cevil
no temeréis.
Remedio en Dios hallaréis
en tanto mal.

Todos:
Pues nos dais vestido nuevo
Rey celestial,
librad de la mala gente
este sayal.

All:
Free this cloth of wool now from
each evil thing.

The Saint:
Since you have come here to die,
have no dismay;
of those in whom evils lie,
no fear display;
remedy find in God's way
for evil thing.

All:
Since you give to us new clothing,
our heavenly King,
free this cloth of wool now from
each evil thing.

Bibliography

The Collected Works of St. John of the Cross. Trans. Kieran Kavanaugh and Otilio Rodriguez. Washington, DC: Institute of Carmelite Studies, 1991. Also available in a CD-ROM from ICS Publications which includes the complete works in Spanish and in English translation by E. Allison Peers.

The Collected Works of St. Teresa of Avila. (3 volumes) Trans. Kieran Kavanaugh and Otilio Rodriguez. Washington, DC: Institute of Carmelite Studies, 1985.

John of the Cross for Today: The Ascent. Susan Muto. Notre Dame, IN: Ave Maria Press, 1991.

John of the Cross for Today: The Dark Night. Susan Muto. Notre Dame, IN: Ave Maria Press, 1994.

Dear Master: Letters on Spiritual Direction Inspired by Saint John of the Cross. Susan Muto. Liguori, MO: Liguori/Triumph, 1999.

Deep into the Thicket. Susan Muto. Pittsburgh, PA: Epiphany Association, 2001.

Words of Wisdom For Our World: The Precautions and Counsels of John of the Cross. Susan Muto. Washington, DC: Institute of Carmelite Studies, 1996.

Ascent To Love: The Spiritual Teaching of St. John of the Cross. Ruth Burrows. Denville, NJ: Dimension Books, 1992.

St. John of the Cross: A Spirituality of Substance. Ed. Peter Slattery, New York: Alba House, 2001.

An Introduction to John of the Cross: When Gods Die. John Welch,
O.Carm. Mahwah, NJ: Paulist Press, 1990.

Spiritual Pilgrims: Carl Jung and Teresa of Avila. John Welch, O.Carm.
Mahwah, NJ: Paulist Press, 1982.

Towards Mystical Union: A modern commentary on the mystical text
The Interior Castle. Julienne McLean. New York: Alba
House, 2003.

Mystical Theology: The Science of Love. William Johnston. Maryknoll,
NY: Orbis Books, 1998.

The Cloud of Unknowing and The Book of Privy Counseling. Anonymous.
Ed. William Johnston. New York: Doubleday, 1973.

Abandonment to Divine Providence. Jean-Pierre de Caussade. Trans.
John Beevers. New York: Doubleday, 1975.

The Practice of the Presence of God. Brother Lawrence. Washington,
DC: Institute of Carmelite Studies, 1994.

The Spiritual Life. Evelyn Underhill. Harrisburg, PA: Morehouse
Publishing, 1937.

Other St. John of the Cross Poetry Translations

The Poems of St. John of the Cross. Trans. Willis Barnstone. New
York: New Directions Publishing Corp., 1972.

St. John of the Cross (San Juan de la Cruz) Alchemist of the Soul. Antonio
T. de Nicolás. York Beach, ME: Samuel Weiser, 1996.

The Poems of St. John of the Cross. Trans. John Frederick Nims.
Chicago: University of Chicago Press, 1989.

The Poems of St. John of the Cross. Trans. Roy Campbell. London:
Harvill Press, 1951.

Loren G. Smith

Loren Smith received his BA degree from Wesleyan University, majoring in Spanish, where he was first introduced to the writings of the great sixteenth century mystics St. Teresa of Avila and St. John of the Cross. After earning his MBA from the Wharton School of the University of Pennsylvania, he pursued a career in business, working for corporations in senior marketing management positions through the 1970's and 1980's.

In 1989, he established his own marketing consulting business which he continues to operate. He also began an in-depth study of the writings of John of the Cross, Teresa and other leading writers in the contemplative tradition. This led to a twelve year project of translating in English verse the poems of John and Teresa.

With the new millennium, he began teaching undergraduate and MBA level marketing courses at Fairfield University and Albertus Magnus College. He is currently serving as Visiting Assistant Professor at Fairfield University.

His marriage of more than forty years has been blessed with two children and five granddaughters.